I JOHN TAKE THEE MARY

I JOHN
TAKE THEE MARY

A BOOK OF CHRISTIAN MARRIAGE

Robert N. Rodenmayer

The Seabury Press
New York

© 1962 by The Seabury Press, Incorporated
Library of Congress Catalog Card Number: 62-12783
Design by Stefan Salter
Printed in the United States of America

394-665-C-12.5-5

Third Printing, June 1965

To my Daughters
Alice
Barbara
Catherine

Preface

It is a rash man who writes yet another book about marriage, but I am prompted to do so for practical reasons. For the past ten years I have taught Pastoral Theology at the Church Divinity School of the Pacific in Berkeley, California, and for almost twenty years before that was a pastor in Episcopal parishes in Massachusetts. In both of these capacities I have had to counsel with men and women before and after their marriages, and for the past decade have tried to teach something about it. During that time I have read a number of helpful books on the subject, for which I am grateful. There are many books on the sexual aspects of marriage, some on its history and sociology, and a great many on its emotional and psychological dimensions. There are novels and plays and poems some of which are more illuminating than the textbooks. But (and this may simply display my ignorance) I have never come upon a satisfying book which I could give to a couple contemplating marriage or to a couple already married and say, "This is what we mean by Christian marriage"—a book which would be free and frank and undefensive and interesting, and yet put the data within a Christian context. So I have tried to write one. I do not pretend to myself that this volume will seem to many any more adequate than some which have seemed inadequate to me, but without some measure of self-regard I suppose that few books would ever have been written. Here then is my offering. It begins with superficial appearances and moves inward; and though the chapter headings indicate some progression, they all overlap and the progress is more in meaning than in time. I write as a priest of the Episcopal Church, but whatever I have to say is applicable to any Christian marriage situation. I think that this is an honest book. I hope that it may be a useful one.

R.N.R.

Berkeley, California
September 1961

Contents

I JOHN TAKE THEE MARY

1 · *The Subject Presented*

MARRIAGE IS AN INTERESTING GAMBLE. PEOPLE HAVE BEEN DO-
ing it for some time now in various ways and with varying
results. Millions of words have been written on the subject
and it is the stock in trade of magazine articles, short story
writers, and Sunday supplements, as well as the theme of
some of the masterpieces of literature. The chief reason for
this, one supposes, is that men and women are the most interesting subject matter we know anything about, and that
together they create the comedies and tragedies, the satis-
factions and the frustrations of life. Not all people are married, or wish to be, but most people are products of marriage
and therefore know something about it. It is the subject
matter closest at hand and one on which anyone can specu-
late without expert knowledge. At the same time it is a
subject matter upon which experts do spend their lives.
In recent years the researches of Dr. Kinsey and his asso-
ciates, along with many others, have raised questions about
marriage in America. We have come to be concerned about
the population explosion in large parts of the world, and we
are worried about the sort of war which might destroy us.

Against this background people continue to fall in love,
get married, have babies, and carry on. No book of this size

can say very much, but it can, perhaps, raise some of the real questions. We shall be thinking about marriage mostly as Americans know it; although this pattern, for better or for worse, is widely adopted. And more deeply than that, we shall be thinking about marriage among Christians. We might begin by looking at some of the findings of our popular instruments of communication, since they are supported by the public and reflect to a large extent what the public thinks.

Taking the average movie, TV serial, or magazine story as a norm, the ideal marriage in America might be described as the right boy marrying the right girl under the right circumstances with the right dreams. Let me expand this sentence, in which you will have noticed that "right" and "ideal" mean the same thing. The simple, sure-fire formula is: Boy meets Girl, Boy loses Girl, Boy gets Girl. But there is a philosophy behind the formula, the philosophy of the American Dream. It goes like this. Once upon a time there was a boy who grew up in Anytown, USA. He may have been bold or shy, handsome or wistful, rich or poor, but he had a good mother and a good heart. In all his callowness, growing-pains, his ups and downs, his successes and failures, his comings and goings, we get the picture of the young American who is sound at the core and ready to take his place in the world as soon as he finds out what it is. In fact, we get an idealized picture of ourselves. This young man engages our sympathies; we like him. Sooner or later he meets the girl who is to be his future wife. He may not know this at the time (though we do, of course) but he knows that she is "special." There are variations on the theme; sometimes he knows in a moment of pure inspiration that this is The One, sometimes it dawns upon him gradually, but there comes a day or a moment when he knows that this is it.

We like the girl for the same reasons. She is good-looking but not glamorous (that's the enemy!), intelligent but still admiring, resourceful but not too independent. She has the well-scrubbed look of good health and she faces the future unafraid. She, too, is an idealized picture of ourselves and we warm to her.

For a while everything goes well for them. Pleasant discovery follows pleasant discovery, friends and families approve, the future is bright with promise, in fact has a certain attractive inevitability about it. Then it happens! It may be that the boy is beguiled momentarily by the glamorous rival whose motives are suspect and who has never had the honest worth of The One. It may be a tragic misunderstanding which, except for some twist of fate (good, this time), might well have wrecked the whole thing. But the episode passes; the boy's eyes are opened, the misunderstanding is explained, the sky is clear again and all is for the best in the best of all possible worlds. Romance has won again, and the downstretch is straight to the altar where the ideally happy couple begin to live happily ever after. The occasion is marked by organ music, candlelight, and simple tears as the well-matched couple exchange their vows and drive off into the well-assured future. The boy is proud and confident; the bride, one of the etiquette books says, should look radiant but not triumphant. And so their good life together begins without spot or wrinkle. Curtain. The End.

Now this is not all bad or undesirable. People do meet and fall in love, they do have misunderstandings and resolve them, they do begin married life with high hopes, and without some hope no marriage would begin at all. But one wonders about the adequacy of the American Dream when one looks at the divorce statistics, or listens to the once happy couple a few years later with the wreckage of their marriage lying about their feet. Is there a more excellent way? Is there a way which admits the attractiveness and, to some extent, the truth of the romantic approach to marriage while at the same time supplying a more realistic insurance against the slings and arrows of outrageous fortune? I think there is, but there is a prior question to be raised.

Why Marry at All?

Certainly there are good reasons for not doing so. Independence, for instance, freedom of movement, quiet when desired without children's clatter and bawling and constant interruptions. The single state is less expensive; the old adage that two can live as cheaply as one is true only if one of them does not eat and the other does not wear clothes. Further, one avoids the tiresome necessity of adjusting to another person's moods and putting up with another person's demands, subtle or imperious. One can have his own circle of friends, go where he chooses, leave when he chooses. A bachelor, it is said, is a person who has never made the same mistake once.

It is true that there are many living alone in this world, some of them liking it more than others. It is true that some seem to be born to become maiden aunts or bachelor uncles, and that some make a fairly satisfactory career of this. It is also true that there are many who wish they were married and are not, especially women—partly because they are not ordinarily expected to do the asking, partly because there are more of them. Marriage would seem to be the normal expectation for people in the Western world. Why is this?

However one chooses to view the process of creation and evolution, our life together is conditioned by the basic fact that some of us are male and others of us are female. It takes the combination of male and female to reproduce one or the other. And if we accept the creation of male and female human beings as a good thing, then it follows that the continuation of the creative process is a good thing. It is a response on the part of living beings to the fact that they are alive, that they have sexual needs, that they wish to reproduce their kind. Added to the basic fact of sexuality in the long development of people and societies (whether families, tribes or nations) is the necessity for order. So we can talk, for instance, of the *history* of marriage and trace its many forms and variations in different times and places. In all of this there are two fundamental observations: sex and society. These are the inescapable constants in our human situation as men and women, however we define their roles.

Within this large framework there are other and perhaps more subtle reasons for marriage. Ortega y Gasset says that genuine love is the attempt to exchange two solitudes. There is much to be said for the bachelor's independence, but it is a lonely business. The price is high. In fact, the price is high either way. The real question is, what do you want to pay for? There is no doubt that one has to pay for loving people; in the long run it is probably the only thing worth paying for. It is not necessary to marry in order to be a whole person but when people do marry they are seeking wholeness.

Meeting Is a Mystery

People often touch but seldom meet. We tend to move in parallel lines, or in social ceremonial patterns, making predictable noises but often with little communication of real feelings. Words are frequently used to keep people apart. How well do you really know anybody—your friend, your neighbor, your child, your husband or wife? In a novel I read recently a woman who had borne her husband eight children was portrayed as thinking reflectively in her husband's presence, "You do not know me, John. You do not know what I am really like at all. You have never taken the trouble to find out."

We really meet in genuine emotions, when we are open. When a couple stand up to be married and say solemnly, looking squarely into each other's eyes, those declarative, committing words, "I John take thee Mary to my wedded Wife, to have and to hold from this day forward," they are communicating simply and truly. It is sometimes the last time that they do so. The key is openness, which is emotionally expensive because it is undefensive. Real fear, hate, love, joy, grief can be felt and spoken, but they can only be received in openness. Only so is there a true meeting. And only so do we really come to know ourselves.

Consider how we come to know those we love best. We meet by arrangement or, more likely, by chance—perhaps at a dance or some other social occasion. Conversation is limited, tentative, exploratory. We tend to fall back on such blessed banalities as the weather, because they fill a conversational silence with something and commit us to nothing. But all the time, beneath the trivia, one is noticing, registering, remembering, projecting. The process is lived through many times, and at any of them a real meeting can take place. Falling in love has been described as a phenomenon of attention. It begins with choice, it is nourished by response.

Gradually we let people in under the guard which we all wear against the world. Gradually we talk about real things, about our families, our other friends. Only after a bit of testing do we talk about our hopes and plans, our dreams. We want to be really heard and it is hard on the young to be laughed at. But when we really *are* heard, really seen, the miracle of meeting has taken place. Two people have been invited into each other's walled garden and have accepted the invitation. Whether this is a genuine but passing summer event, the start of a life-long friendship, or the beginning of a friendship which ripens into love and marriage, this is the nature of our real life together. Somewhere down this road, though not immediately, is the treasure of shared silence, the complement of the ability to speak and be heard. This is silence in depth, the opposite of the brittle and nervous silence of those first encounters. After the miracle of meeting has deepened and blossomed, these people might sit for hours in front of a fireplace or walk for miles in a misty rain or lie in bed together, and it would not matter whether they spoke or not. They would be free to share the words or the silence and there would be a communion.

But this involves real people in real situations, not the glamorized cut-outs of the American Dream boy-meets-girl situation. The bachelor may choose to remain so, but it is a pity when he so chooses while legally married. We have been duped by our own myth of "independence," but even more have we been duped by the romantic dream of love and marriage on a pink cloud where the prince marries the princess and they live together happily ever after. Nothing has to be worked out; everything is there, everything is perfect. And when imperfections begin to show, the Great Disillusion sets in and the project is abandoned. One has been promised a prize which somehow he didn't get.

A Union of All Things Excellent

In contrast, here are some interesting and honest words which were written by Jeremy Taylor, an Anglican bishop of the 17th century.

The first blessing God gave to man was a society, and that society was a marriage, and that marriage was confedèrate by God Himself and hallowed by a blessing . . . This state hath proper exercises and trials for those graces for which single life can never be crowned; here is the proper scene of piety and patience, of the duty of parents and the charity of relatives; here kindness is spread abroad and love is united and made firm as a centre. Marriage is the nursery of heaven . . . the state of marriage fills up the number of the elect and hath in it the labor of love and the delicacies of friendship, the blessing of society and the union of hands and hearts. It hath in it less of beauty but more of safety than the single life, it hath more care but less danger, it is more merry and more sad, it is fuller of sorrows and fuller of joys; it lies under more burdens but is supported by all the strength of love and charity, and those burdens are delightful. Marriage is the mother of the world and preserves kingdoms and fills cities and churches and heaven itself . . . She who is loved is safe, he who loves is joyful . . . Love is a union of all things excellent; it contains in it proportion and satisfaction and rest and confidence.

The American Dream about love and marriage is a romantic escape—from responsibility and therefore from meaning—which in turn derives from a twelfth-century escape of a similar sort when Romanticism was born in the days of chivalry in Southern France. This tradition of the knight who slays dragons, frees cities, overcomes evil with his bright sword, to be rewarded by his (unreal and unreachable) lady's smile—this tradition is deeply grained into our folklore, our literature and our thinking. Even the "Western" perpetuates the formula: our hero having dealt masterfully with the forces of evil rides off into the sunset. There is a girl of course (who sometimes has a father but never a mother) who is milady; the hero kisses her hand but never marries her. In fact, they never meet except as romantic symbols. They never discover unpleasant things about each other except as an early misunderstanding inevitably cleared up as the hero and the dragon identify themselves and one another in this tidy, never-never land of Goods and Bads.

Now it would be a mistake and a loss to believe that the romantic dream is useless. It has many uses, but two in particular. First, it enriches life and adds a dimension of imagination.

> I should like to rise and go
> Where the golden apples grow.

Don Quixote and his grandly ridiculous windmills, Yeats sailing to Byzantium, are an irreplaceable part of our cultural landscape and we would be poorer without them, a part of us unfed. Also, the romantic dream is a starter, an incentive. No man would ever set out for El Dorado or the

New World or the Good Society had he not dreamed about it first. Few would enter into marriage without hope, and the dream sustains the hope. "Where there is no vision the people perish." The difficulty comes in confusing dream with reality, in making a romantic phoney of the best thing we have been given—a real, loving, responsive, deeply satisfying relationship between two flesh and blood human beings who meet each other freely, gladly and honestly in all departments of living. In such a union there is room for romance and laughter, for shared sorrow and compassion and thanksgiving and growth.

Jessamyn West says, wisely:

"Falling in love," like love itself, comes by grace. One may be ready for it; one may feel that one's whole life is a readying for it. But "falling in love" courted as an end makes one a drug addict, an addict disastrously able to manufacture his own toxins and with neither law nor economics to stand between him and his own destruction. Nothing can save him except his determination to live his life instead of dream it. Why should one live one's life instead of dream it? For the reason that one cannot dream a life. One can only dream a dream. A life must be lived. A dream of love remains a dream. A life of love is a life. Love is a lived dream. And such a living, by the testimony of all, those who have failed in it and those who have succeeded, constitutes the only completely satisfying existence in the world.°

For more centuries than anyone can tell, the interesting dissimilarities between men and women have been noted and published. So far as I know, the first person to remark about wives, that it was impossible to live with one in comfort and equally impossible to live at all without one, was

° Jessamyn West, *Love Is Not What You Think.* (New York: Harcourt, Brace, 1959), p. 14.

Q. Caecilius Metellus, censor in 131 B.C., in a speech before the Roman Senate. These differences have been the source of many jokes—since humor is partly a way of venting frustration—and have furnished the background for some of the world's great writing.

It has often been observed that a man has two focal points in his life, his woman and his job in the world, while a woman has but one. Her home is her life and her job in the world. The man needs the woman but not all of the time; there are worlds to be conquered, causes to be served, many things to be done outside the circumference of this home. There are many disappointed women who do not know this, or who refuse to accept it. Byron says,

> Man's love is of man's life a thing apart;
> 'Tis woman's whole existence.

A man's deepest need is to be involved, caught up, important to a cause, an enterprise, even a routine. A woman's deepest need is to be needed. Man surpasses woman in his capacity for friendship, is surpassed by her in the capacity for love. A woman in love is *there* completely.

A Strange, New World

These things are mysteries, but they are supposed to be. Our deepest wisdom is to know that we are surrounded by mystery. It is the beginning of all art and all science. It is our ability to wonder, to be amazed, to be completed—at least momentarily—by discovery. Men and women in their different ways make voyages into the mystery of love and marriage, but they can never penetrate its secrets. It would be a tragedy if they could.

There be three things which are too wonderful for me, yea, four which I know not: The way of an eagle in the air; the way of a serpent upon a rock; the way of a ship in the midst of the sea; and the way of a man with a maid. (*Proverbs 30:18-19*)

No, the mystery remains and will remain. On the working level there is some choice as to how it is to be approached. Let us go back for a moment to the tentative, exploratory process of meeting. Here the solitudes, the private worlds are open for the other to explore. One is delighted to find a shared emotion, a common response to a poem, a person, an event. It is the beginning of community, the possibility of a shared home. Competition is there but so also is completion. Acquaintance ripens into friendship nourished by shared experience, by the pleasure of approaching things and people together as this man and this woman, and the pleasure of knowing the experience together afterwards. So the process of knowing goes on, like children coming home from a day at the seaside with sticky hands full of treasures. A strange new world has been seen, filling the mind with wonder.

There are places in our lives which we cannot share, even if we should like to do so. They may be guessed at, sometimes wrongly, but they cannot be invaded. But the adventure of discovery goes on for a lifetime if the marriage is real, always tenderly, always with courtesy. We need to respect each other's privacy and to deal tenderly with each other's dreams. Some years ago a college girl, now happily married and the mother of a growing family, wrote these words: "Love is an outgoing sense of exceeding good will directed toward another person. It combines a feeling of fellowship and adoration, sustenance and splendor. Love is not a retreat from the hard things of life but a citadel from which to gain strength to meet the complex problems of a public and private world." This is not only a vision (though at the time it was mostly that), it is a truth to be lived out. When it is a shared thing, that marriage—no matter what troubles and griefs there may be—will be strong and good. When it is not shared or when it is scorned, the vision will not die but it will shrink to a small, bright, hidden place, to be remembered with sadness. A richness has become a poverty. It may be true in the main that sacrifice is feminine while forgiveness is masculine, but both are needed by both and for both all the time.

The differences between men and women are a part of the "impossibility" remarked by Metellus and at the same time they are the possibility in this created world of a real meeting place for a man and a woman in all aspects of their life together. They can be admitted, welcomed and explored, or feared, hated and refused. We shall think about them in various ways in the chapters to come. Meanwhile, we shall remember that marriage is for grown-up people, of whatever chronological age. It is not only a dream, it is a life, a "lived dream." It is a society, a home, an adventure, a trust, a hope, a reality. It is probably the best thing that men and women can know on this earth.

2 · Problems

THERE ARE NO IDEAL MARRIAGES BUT THERE ARE MANY GOOD ones. There is no such thing as an ideal mate waiting to be discovered but there are many persons to whom one might be well married. There is no marriage which does not require adjustments, a shakedown cruise, but it is the part of common sense that a couple might hopefully begin with as many things as possible in their favor. In other times and places marriages were arranged by parents, or by marriage brokers who made their living that way. Young people nowadays find such a proceeding repugnant; partly because they wish to make such a choice independently and partly because of our romantic ideal. To modern sensibilities an arranged marriage smacks of a business deal, cold and impersonal, or perhaps a horse trade. Actually there is much to be said for the system. Some basic compatibilities may be matched up, the roles of the respective families defined, a sound economic footing established. But, we say, we prefer to make our own mistakes. We prefer to fall in love with the romantic ideal. We hope to be permanently exalted (which never happens) and to escape being cruelly disillusioned (which we often are). Again, the question presents itself: is there some way other than blind chance in which a compromise can be brought about between romanticism and common sense?

I have said that I think there is. Our usual procedure is to become physically attracted to a person whom we then invest with ideal qualities for which there may or may not be justification. It would seem prudent at this point in the relationship, even in terms of intelligent self-interest, to raise some questions as to community of interests and the ability to meet in ways other than the purely romantic. What does one talk about between periods of romancing? What are the chances that this couple may be truly married seven years or seventeen years from the day when they said the words? Are there hidden strains or cross-purposes which under pressure might destroy the marriage? What will they have to contribute as a couple to the society around them?

Two Basic Questions

None of these questions can be "answered"; however they can be predicted to some extent. To that end let me raise two basic questions under which a number of others may cluster. What are the important things for a couple to know about each other before marriage? What should one know about oneself? The second may well provide a direction for the first. What am I looking for in marriage? What is marriage going to provide for me that nothing else can? A home? An escape? A sexual convenience? A family? A security? A companionship? Some of all of these? And, if so, in what sort of priority? What is my role in this marriage, and what is my partner's? What will this marriage cost in terms of self-limitation? Marriage, we sometimes hear, is a fifty-fifty proposition; the fact is, it is not a proposition at all. It is a life to be lived out in close proximity and in intimate relationship with another life. Marriage is not so much a cement as it is a solvent, a freeing-up of this man and this woman to be themselves and to help each other in the process of self-discovery. So the two questions are not as separate as they seem on first reading. Growth in knowledge of oneself goes on most helpfully with other people.

Sometimes the root questions can be best approached by way of practicalities. Let us try it that way. Here is a list of twenty-five questions for people contemplating marriage, arranged in categories.

The Marriage Service

1. Have you read the service, so that you know what it says about Christian marriage and what you are to promise?
2. Are you planning your wedding as you yourselves wish it, so that you will always cherish the memory of it?
3. Have you considered others, particularly your parents and relatives, in deciding who will be present at it?

Your Religion

4. Are you members of the same Church?
5. Have you ever talked together of your ideas of God, or of what it means to be a Christian?
6. Does the Church to which you belong meet your spiritual needs?
7. What part will the public worship of the Church play in your lives?
8. If you are not members of the same Church, have you seriously studied each other's religion to find out if you might unite on one Church?

9. If not, have you counted the cost of a divided loyalty and intelligently faced it?
10. Do you pray regularly? Ever?

Interests

11. What interests have you in common? Have you considered how you will develop them?
12. What separate interests, hobbies, or obligations have you which might take time (evenings and holidays) or money from what you might otherwise spend together? Have you considered together the continuation of these activities?

Finances

13. Do you know what your total income will be?
14. How much of this income will be spent in starting housekeeping, your wedding, or paying off debts?
15. Have you budgeted your income so that you know how much you will need for rent, food, fuel, clothing, doctors, recreation, "good will" (that is, donations, gifts, organization dues, etc.) and savings?
16. Have you any relatives who are, or might become, wholly or temporarily dependent upon you? Does the other realize this?

Parents and In-laws

17. Is either of you over-dependent on parents, or inconsiderate of them or of in-laws?
18. Is there any feeling of tension with parents or in-laws which could be cleared up at this time with a friendly, frank talk?
19. Does either of you feel restrained by the other in carry-

ing out what you feel to be your rightful and loving
obligations to your family?

20. Are there any particular circumstances of sickness,
loneliness, or isolation that will necessitate either of you
being with your parents a great deal? If so, does the
other realize this?

21. Are conditions such that at any time you might have to
live with relatives, or they with you? If so, do you both
understand this?

Personal Questions

22. Is there anything in marriage which you fear? Do you
fear yourself? Each other? The finality of marriage?
Do you fear having children, or any of the other physical aspects of marriage?

23. Have you, to your own knowledge, any disease, or likelihood of disease, which might affect your future? Have
you seen a reliable doctor in regard to this?

24. Is there anything in the life of either of you which you
have concealed, or intend to conceal from the other?

25. Is there any information which you do not possess, and
feel you should have before you are married?

Honest answers to such questions will begin to disclose
some of the real issues. How free are these persons to marry
anyone? Are they willing and able to commit themselves
to one another, for better or for worse, or are there reservations? If there are reservations, are they such as can be offered to one another? Are they marrying one another in an
act of acceptance and faith, or for what they hope to make
of each other? What is really valuable to each of these peo-

ple? What would each of them hate most to lose? Is there such egotism in either party that that person is incapable of accepting the marriage bond, or of loving? Is there incapability of allowing oneself to be loved? Is there a constitutional insecurity in one party? If so, is the other person willing or able to offer the needed assurance? Does either party have a career attitude that does not allow him to marry? Is marriage simply a way to a career? Is either person so adolescent that he is incapable of freedom from his family? What is the passive-aggressive pattern of these people? Will there be so much competition for role that life will be unbearable?

An Offering of Steady Regard

I am sure that one of the basic issues in contemplating marriage centers around the word respect—the ability to regard another person favorably quite apart from oneself. Real marriage is the union of two free persons, it is larger than the sum of its parts. Respect for another person is the bestowal of personhood upon him. He or she is not an ego-extension, a person one devours or controls, but a person in his own right to whom one relates. Respect is an offering of one's steady regard. It presupposes integrity on both parts and a willingness to trust. It presupposes honesty on both parts and willingness to be found wrong. For only those to whom we are open can hurt us. Consider encountering a person in the street whom you have never seen before, who says to you, "I think you are a fool." Nothing is likely to happen. You might be surprised or curious or shocked, or concerned for the speaker, but you would not be hurt, probably not even touched, because the words are those of a stranger. You might well think him odd but you would not have to listen.

Now consider that your closest friend, one with whom you have been through all sorts of things both happy and sad, says to you, "John, old man, I think you are making a fool of yourself." No matter what your immediate reaction is, your inner question would be, What do you mean? Because of the relationship between you his remark cannot go disregarded; it cannot simply be brushed off as the meaningless remark of a stranger. Whatever the momentary defenses may be, the opinion of your old friend will have to be considered and probably pursued. So with respect; it confers the right to have an opinion and to speak it. It involves a willingness to hear, to be criticized. If such an attitude is present before a marriage begins, the chances for its successful ripening into a deep and creative union will be immeasurably increased. The absence of such a willingness is a danger signal.

What we are talking about, of course, is the degree to which these persons contemplating marriage are grown up. The state of grown-up-ness or emotional maturity includes, among other things, the ability to form free and independent decisions; the ability to see that such decisions might be wrong; and the freedom to admit failure when they prove to be wrong. It also includes the ability to allow the other person to be grown-up in this same manner.

How does one go about determining this quality in a future mate? I am not sure, but I do know that it is one of the most important questions to raise, and there are some ways of noticing if we are alert to them. How does this person react when everything goes wrong? So often in the days of our courtship we are at pains to appear at our best. We are quick to serve, to respond, to agree, to admire. But how is the temper when there is a flat tire on the way to the party for which one is already a little late, and it is raining? What is the emotional climate when one's dearest opinions are challenged in public and perhaps disastrously refuted? What happens when the manager-type woman is opposed, or when the sweet one is tired?

In a devastatingly honest little book, *He Sent Leanness,** David Head addresses himself to the subject of courtship and marriage in the prayers of the natural man:

May we find marriage the end of all our problems, and live happily ever after.
May he have no secrets, and never discover mine.
May she be always useful and always beautiful, full of interesting conversation, witty in private and sparkling in public, blind to my faults, tolerant with my follies, never weary, never demanding, enjoying her own company when necessary, not getting too involved with female friends, performing miracles with her housekeeping allowance, and always grateful that I married her.

To Laugh and to Cry

The problem is one of real persons really meeting. No one can be sweet or calm or reasonable all the time, though we all pretend a lot. And it does require a measure of maturity to be willing to be caught out. It is emotionally expensive, yet it is one of the chief ingredients of a successful marriage.

Humor is an index to compatibility. If you were to think

* David Head, *He Sent Leanness.* (New York: The Macmillan Co., 1959).

for a minute or two of the persons whose company you enjoy most I think you might find that they are the men or women with whom you enjoy laughter, the sense of the ridiculous. There is a further compatibility between those who think the same things are funny. Life is a tragi-comedy in which there are occasions when we laugh in order that we may not weep. But it is not a series of guffaws, and one feels sad for the professionals who have to work for their living at being funny. I am thinking of a different kind of humor, a gentler kind. There is a quiet smile of shared understanding, a sparkling smile of shared delight. There is a shy smile of offered friendship, and a wry smile at one's own discomfiture. And here is the occasional uproarious, side-splitting releasing laughter at some shared event so ridiculously absurd that it draws tears.

The ability to laugh and to cry is one of the marks which distinguishes human beings from the other animals. It is the ability to enter into life, to feel and to share joys and sorrows. And this sharing of lights and shadows, this ability to live both above and below the flat surface of things within the compass of a marriage companionship is one of the greatest gifts of life. Choose a man or woman with whom you can share laughter; it will never put money in the bank for you but it will ease many a rough place along the way.

Standard Problems

A standard question consistently raised by young people in groups discussing courtship and marriage is that about The One. It usually turns up something like this. Suppose you meet this wonderful boy and after a while you decide to get married. Maybe you have been married for a few months or a few years when you meet the person you really should have married in the first place. You just *know* it. Whenever you look at him you turn to jelly and you wonder what you ever saw in the man you married. Compared to this real one he is as dull and uninteresting as a faded photograph. What a dilemma. What does one do now? In many stories or movies you would explain to your husband more or less kindly that this is it, you never really loved him, your true love has appeared and you are going away with him forever. After all, what are the other choices? A life of bondage served out in boredom? A life of grim pretense with few compensations and many private tears?

There is no use in our pretending that this sort of thing does not happen; and when it does there is no easy answer because the problem is not easy. A direct and honest answer might have to be to stick it out, live it out. You took this person in good faith, for better or for worse, so stop acting like a child and live with your choice. The trouble is that the question is not usually presented, before the decision is made, to a person who would answer it this way. The question is more likely to be raised, if at all, among one's close friends of the same sex and the answer—straight out of the serials —will probably be to follow your heart.

It may be clear by now what I think about this problem. While courtship is a romantic period in anyone's life, it may also be a realistic one, and if the marriage is to last and grow it will have to be. The real questions are not about hair and eyes or Junes and moons, though without such attractions the couple perhaps would not have met. The real questions have to do with who we are and how much we have to go on, with what we believe in and trust, with respect and grown-up-ness, with tears and laughter shared, with two lives slowly and quietly being knit together in tenderness and strength. The attractive stranger will appear. He or she always does—and more than once. The question rises, is there room for him? Hopefully, the marriage will be full enough of its own living not to be vulnerable. There is no guarantee of this, no secret formula. It does take more than the romantic dream to make a marriage, but the other material is at hand, too.

Another standard problem is that of the mixed marriage, religiously or racially or both. Much has been written on this subject recently and some of it is very helpful. I raise it in our chapter on problems in order to ask some questions of those who may be facing it personally. The first question has to do with the emotional maturity of the parties involved. How much can they bear? Any marriage relationship demands emotional maturity; a mixed marriage needs more than the average degree of it. More than the usual problems will have to be faced in advance. What about the children, for instance? If this is an inter-faith marriage which way will the children go, and on whose option? Are they likely to become a battle ground for the in-laws? It would appear that the chances of a marriage surviving are increased when the husband and wife belong to the same religious body. If they decide to go their separate ways, a good marriage is still possible but not without considerable respect and understanding and love. The problem of the children should be settled before they are born, and to the quiet satisfaction of both parents.

In an inter-racial marriage the problem of the children will depend to some extent on the nature of the community, and the variations are extreme. In some large cities or in some academic communities there might be little question.

Our whole country is in process of change on this issue and it will take a while. There is no theological problem about inter-racial marriages since God created people, all of them. But there are problems of living in different places in a changing society and the responsibility for bringing up children in them. Even for the couple themselves there are serious questions in advance. What doors will be closed that used to be open? And what about the in-laws, when they may represent quite different cultures? What difference will it make in employment, religious practice, possible places in which to live? Statistics indicate that mixed marriages in general have less chance of lasting than those with fewer emotional problems. They can be successful; it takes a lot more doing.

The question of in-laws in general depends on two factors. The first is the accepted finding that, at least in the Western world as contrasted with some Oriental and Near-Eastern cultures, three generations do not get along very well together, especially in the same house. The other factor is the individuals themselves, what they are like and, to a lesser extent, the living conditions. Young couples want to be on their own and need to be, especially in those cases, for instance, when a mother has great difficulty in letting her son go to be taken care of by another (and less able!) woman. Such a couple, looking the facts in the eye, may have to move, and a long way. Even so it may not be far enough and from time to time a declaration of independence and of new loyalty will have to be stated. On the other hand many times a grandmother or grandfather turns out to be a blessing in many ways—not only such practical advantages as free baby-sitting, but as members of the household who enrich its whole life. There is a great advantage, however, in having some independence. Ideally, everyone needs the privilege of being able to close a door when he wants to be alone. This is not always possible, but how much more desirable when more than one generation is living in the same house, and for each of them!

People of both sexes in America live longer than they used to and old people are an increasing element in our general population. Many wise heads are concerning themselves with possible solutions, and one thing seems pretty clear: older people on the whole prefer the company of their own contemporaries, especially if from time to time they can make sorties to visit their children and grandchildren and leave when they please. It often happens that even a much-beloved grandmother would prefer to live in a home for older people, if it is a good one.

The long engagement is less of a problem than it used to be in that it occurs less frequently. Couples tend to marry younger, and on shorter notice. This is not necessarily to be deplored, yet the old-fashioned, long engagement was sometimes useful for getting acquainted and exchanging views, not infrequently by correspondence. But the extent to which people come to know each other depends less on length of time than on the degree of openness. If their lines of communication are open now for the expression of real feelings, they may well remain so.

3 · The Wedding

THE DAY OF THE WEDDING IS A GREAT DAY. THE PROPOSAL HAS been made and accepted, the astonishing proposition has become a reality. Now the date has been set, public and private plans all flow in the same direction, like a stream picking up speed before a cascade. There is no other public occasion quite like it. The family lives through days and weeks of speculation and misgivings, appointments and disappointments, emotional upheavals and moments of welcome quiet, clothes and presents, rehearsals and dinners. Finally the day arrives. Somehow the cast is assembled, the music rolls, the words are spoken and the deed is done. It hardly seems possible.

Reactions are various. The father of the bride is proud of his daughter, misses her, is glad the thing is over. The bride's mother shares this but has rather enjoyed the whole business and, mysteriously, she feels less sense of loss as the car drives away because, after all, she is the girl's mother and there is a secret understanding which they will always share. The groom's parents have parallel feelings though at a greater remove from the scene of action.

The bride and groom are launched. After the days of

waiting and the last-minute bustle of activity the ceremony itself seemed brief and solemn. The photographs, the receiving line, the reception, the flurry of the leave-taking—all blur together pleasantly. Now they are alone together and rather quiet. They are a new thing, a married couple. This is their new life beginning, and they are thinking about themselves and each other. Just what is it that they have done? They seem to have done a great many things recently, leading up to this public ceremony, but at the heart of it they have made a contract and received a blessing.

The essence of a marriage contract is an agreement between a man and a woman to live together as man and wife, to assume responsibility for each other, for property held in common and for any children who may issue from this union. Actually the couple marry one another; they are the high contracting parties. The function of the witnesses is to testify that they were present at the time and place of the making of the contract and heard the words spoken. The function of the clergyman is a double one: he acts as an official recognized by the state as a person properly qualified to join couples in the marriage bond, and as an official recognized by the Church to bless this man and this woman in the name of God, and to invoke the prayers of the congregation in their behalf. In the words of The Book of Common Prayer this is called "The Solemnization of Matrimony." The two recordings are indications of this double role. The marriage is recorded, with the clergyman's signature, both in the town or city clerk's office and in the parish register; the proceeding is governed both by civil and by canon law. In some countries all marriages are civil contracts; and if the couple wish to signify their intention that their marriage shall be a Christian one, then they make proper arrangements for a religious ceremony. As we shall see this is a reversion to a much earlier custom.

Here is an interesting summary of a large amount of data on the background of this event.

Marriage is an institution of the natural order, the primary significance of which lies in its causal, not casual, relation to the family. The history of human marriage is the story of the evolution of the family as the primary social group and the basis of whatever degree of civilization has as yet been achieved by the human race. After promiscuity, polygamy and every other conceivable relationship of the sexes has been tried and found wanting, monogamous marriage, the lifelong union of one man and one woman, is found to be the highest and socially the most valuable union of the sexes; highest, because even its tensions make for patience and strength of character; socially the most valuable, because in it the interests of the children are best secured and because the welfare of the child is essential to human progress.

If one uses the word natural in its full and deep sense, with regard for the meaning of history and the well-nigh universal verdict of human experience, it may be asserted that monogamy is the only natural form of marriage. The deep-rooted sentiments, conjugal and paternal, upon which it is based may be regarded as the very voice of uncorrupted nature bearing eternal witness to its significance.

To this voice of nature human society adds corroboration. It expresses and to some extent maintains its own great interests. When a man and a woman come together to assume the relation of husband and wife, their marriage is more than a private relation between individuals. It has created a new social organism, the organism of the family, which like all other organisms is greater than its parts. The relation between the individuals has ceased to be a mere matter of contract and has become a status created by contract. A family has come into being.°

Sources of the Marriage Rite

Let us retrace a bit. Marriage both as a rite and as a state of life is not something peculiarly Christian but rather is an institution of the natural order which is taken into and sanctified by the Christian Church. How did this come about? The marriage service as we know it (I shall assume the text of the service as it occurs in The Book of Common Prayer as a norm) has two general sources. One, the main one, is the marriage customs of pre-Christian Rome; the other is Germanic. For approximately the first thousand years of Christian history there was no such thing as a "Marriage Service." There were any number of local secular forms or usages all centering around the essential contract, which was signified by joining hands. It is true that in Jewish custom the bridegroom simply acknowledged his bride in public, and that in pre-Christian Teutonic culture the contract was between the father of the bride and the bridegroom; but in all cases the contract was primary. The Church did not concern itself with the manner in which the contract was made but with the married parties themselves. It was not

° For this quotation (pp. 4-5) and for the organization of much of the following historical material I am indebted to an out-of-print book, *The Bond of Honour*, written in 1938 by two of my former teachers, Burton Scott Easton and Howard Chandler Robbins, and to The Macmillan Company for permission to use it.

until the Twelfth Century that it became customary for clergymen to officiate at wedding ceremonies. However, it was a widespread early Christian custom for the newly married couple to go to church for a blessing, to present offerings and to make their communions. This custom became almost universal, thus marking a distinction between the marriage itself, which was the act of the parties, and the blessing which was the act of the Church.

Among us the engagement of a couple to be married is usually a private affair but it was not always so. In pre-Christian Rome the betrothal was a public act, an interchange of promises to marry each other, and the promise was sealed with a pledge by the man of his willingness to share his property with his future wife. This pledge usually took the form of jewelry, as a convenience, and, as early as the Second Century before the Christian era, was normally a ring.

The other source of our present rite is the customs of the Germanic tribes among which women were regarded as property, and the marriage as a transfer of ownership from the father to the husband. With the conversion of the Teutons to Christianity women won the right to act as individuals. Custom was strong enough, however, to require that the bride have a temporary guardian to represent her father's rights, and for this purpose the parish priest was a natural choice. In this way the clergyman began to take an active part in both betrothal and wedding, until by the Fourteenth Century canon law began to declare marriages invalid unless performed by a priest. Our custom of the "giving away" of the bride by her father derives similarly from a modification of the old property right. The practice represents the father giving his daughter to the Church, in the person of the priest, and of the priest in his capacity of temporary guardian bestowing her upon the bridegroom.

So the occasions of betrothal and wedding came to be joined as parts of a single ceremony in that they were usually performed by the same person, the bride's pastor. In our rite the betrothal serves as an introduction to the marriage. Interestingly, the giving of the ring was transferred to the wedding proper and the custom of an "engagement ring" grew up to take the place of the former betrothal pledge. The result is our familiar practice of the bride's having two rings.

The Role of the Pastor

When a couple decide to be married, they will normally make a visit to their pastor to talk things over. There are a number of reasons for this. In the first place he probably knows at least one of them quite well and will be affectionately concerned in their hopes and plans. He is the person who will officiate at the wedding, for both Church and State. And he is the person who, by reason of training and experience, is equipped to counsel with them about the nature of the marriage relationship. It is both courteous and sensible for a couple to make their call on the pastor very soon after they have become engaged. There is, for example, the matter of possible dates and all sorts of practical details, quite apart from the fact that this is the person who can probably be of the greatest help now and later on. A number of church bodies, among them the Episcopal Church, require a counseling session as a prerequisite to the marriage. In any case there will have to be a meeting to determine whether or not the pastor is legally, canonically (if his church is so governed), and morally free to officiate at the marriage. Both common sense and good will prompt many pastors to arrange pre-marital interviews on the nature of this responsibility, even though not formally required to do so.

The number and the nature of the counseling sessions before the wedding will depend upon the pastor's willingness and ability, how busy he is, and where this sort of thing comes in his own priority of values. One would hope that it might be an important concern since it can be helpful not only in giving out information but, more important, in establishing attitudes and in providing a basis on which future meetings may be held if necessary. The pastor might use a set of questions, such as those in the previous chapter, as a starting place for the first interview. If not, it is important that the couple themselves do so, and for their own reasons. It is quite possible that he will use the marriage service itself as an outline for the meeting. No matter what the outline is, it is important that these persons will have seriously considered the promises they are about to make, and their implications. Let us do so now. In The Book of Common Prayer the service begins on page 300.

The Promises

The prefatory address sets the stage for the action that is to follow. It states the reason for the meeting, the joining of this man and this woman in holy matrimony, and goes on to describe that state as honorable, instituted of God (that is, occurring in the natural order), and adopted and sanctified by the Church, as witnessed by a reference in *Ephesians* and by the fact that the Lord took part in a wedding at Cana, as described in the *Gospel According to St. John.* Therefore it is a serious and not a casual proceeding which is about to take place; and because this transaction is important not only to the principals but to society at large, an opportunity is provided for any citizen to state why it should not proceed. And the final admonition—if just cause cannot be shown now why this wedding should not take place, let it not be brought up later.

This introduction to the marriage service has been both shorter and longer in the history of the Church, but its intent has always been the same. The prefatory address is of North European origin rather than Roman and was formalized chiefly in York and Salisbury. Some might be interested in the old York form:

"Lo, brethren, we are come here before God and His angels and all His Saints, in the face and presence of our mother, holy Church, for to couple and knit these two bodies together, that is to say, of this man and this woman, that they be from this time forth but one body and two souls in the faith and law of God and holy Church, for to deserve everlasting life, whatsoever they have done here before.

"I charge you on God's behalf and holy Church, that if there be any of you that can say anything why these two may not lawfully be wedded together at this time, say it now either privily or openly, in helping of your souls and theirs both."

And to the bride and groom:

"Also I charge you both, and either by yourself, as you will answer before God at the day of doom, that if there be anything done privily or openly between yourselves, or that you know any lawful hindrance why that you may not be wedded together at this time, say it now ere we do any more to this matter."

There follow the betrothal promises. Once separate from the actual wedding, they still have a semi-independent position and are exchanged at the foot of the chancel steps. They look to the future and though some of their words are shared with those of the contract itself, the betrothal promises have the character of taking a long look forward through the arches of the years. The operating words are four verbs: love, comfort, honor, keep.

The question is sometimes raised quite honestly how one can promise to love another person a number of years from now. I shall have something to say about the source and maintenance of Christian love in the next chapter, but I should like to make two general observations now. The first is that the rather elusive word love finds all of its expressions in a good marriage. These people were once acquaintances who became friends; later they became lovers in the usual sense, and perhaps parents. They may become companions and realize a fellowship which grows deeper with years and events. Looking back over many years of married life they can say that it has been good and include in that statement a whole spectrum of thoughts and feelings; moments of ecstasy, jewel-like memories of special events, griefs and disappointments, and the familiar rhythm of the daily round. My second observation is that love in this sense is more than sensation though sensation may be included in it. Rather, it is a steady attitude of good will directed toward another person. This sort of love is not dependent upon sensation or special events. It is an affectionate open regard in good times and bad and it can be promised in advance because it is not dependent upon how one feels at any given moment. Love in many of our popular songs and stories is almost completely sensational, its end purpose being to provoke responsive feelings in another man or woman. The love of a Christian is more generous, less like looking into a mirror. It confers a right, a privilege, a dignity on the loved one whether there is a response or not. It lives by being given away. Being free it makes free response possible.

To comfort, in the sense in which it is used here, means to strengthen rather than to soothe; to build up, support, sustain. It follows on from our consideration of love. A clear-eyed regard for another person will perceive that person's needs and a way to meet them. It need not be dramatic. Mrs. Miniver says the nicest thing about marriage is an eye to catch. A smile can be sustaining, and a readiness to let another person be seen and heard can be a support.

Something should be said, I think, for the current use of the word comfort; it, too, has a place in marriage. A hurt child needs to be comforted by loving arms and words and sent back to the business of living. So also those of us who are no longer children need occasionally, and sometimes very much indeed, the comfort of loving understanding and sympathy when we have been hurt. No young couple standing up to say these words can know what lies ahead of them in the changes and chances of their life together, and it is well that they do not; but they may know that there will be many times when they will need one another's comfort and compassion. The promise is a good one even though imperfectly understood, for compassion (which has to be learned slowly and at personal expense) is one of the genuine fruits of a good marriage.

To honor is to respect, about which we have already had

some thoughts. This man and this woman are different persons, each with his own personal history up to this moment, promising now so to entwine their lives and purposes that they may become one. But their separateness will remain and should remain that it may be offered each to the other again and again. This can happen only in an atmosphere of respect, each knowing the other as different, having somewhat different lacks, needing completion.

To keep, in sickness and in health (a phrase soon to be repeated before the altar) is the real answer to the question about meeting the real One later. Among all the people these two might have married they have chosen each other, and are now promising to live out their lives together whatever may happen in the days and years ahead. When we use the verb "to keep" in ordinary speech (Will you keep this for me, please?) we mean to put something in a safe place—"safe keeping." It is the same in this exchange of promises. The loved one is safe, the keeping is secure. An honorable man keeps a promise, a loving one keeps a person.

The wedding contract differs from the betrothal promises chiefly in point of time. The one says, "I will," and looks to the future. The other says now, ". . . from this day forward, for better for worse, for richer for poorer, in sickness and in health, to love and to cherish, till death us do part . . ." Thus the agreement is made and publicly witnessed, forever. No two persons can ever make a more solemn pact and, no matter what light-hearted occasions may have gladdened the wedding festivities, these words pronounced deliberately after the officiating clergyman are sobering. This is the quiet place between the bustle of the rehearsal and the good cheer of the reception, the essential moment. Here two lives are joined and wedded by common consent. Here a new social unit comes into being. Here a man and woman become a husband and a wife.

The seal of the contract and its sign, as long as they live, is a ring given and received. The old Sarum (Salisbury) form is interesting: "With this ring I thee wed, and this gold and silver I give thee, and with my body I thee worship, and with all my worldly cathel I thee endow." The first recorded instance where a clergyman officiated at a wedding (he blessed the ring) was in 856 when King Ethelwulf married Judith, daughter of Charles the Bald. In our rite the ring is blessed, as then, as a symbol of the intention of the marriage. The words in The Book of Common Prayer are: "Bless, O Lord, this ring, that he who gives it and she who wears it may abide in thy peace, and continue in thy favour, unto their life's end; through Jesus Christ our Lord."

There follows the Lord's Prayer (the first words spoken by the newly married couple) and three other prayers: for the marriage, for the gift of children, and for the new home. Finally, the declaration of the marriage and the blessing. The promises have been spoken, the contract made. The prayers of the congregation have been invoked and the couple have been blessed in the name of the Lord. Whatever happens to them now happens to *them*, for they are man and wife.

Note:

A word about fees may be helpful. There should be no such thing as a fee for a clergyman officiating at a wedding when it is done within the context of the Christian community. It is a family act, for and by the family. However, it is entirely appropriate for a newly married couple to make a gift, a thank-offering, for what they have received. Also if one has required special services from organist, sexton, or altar guild it is not unreasonable to find that they have stand-ard fees. Church organists are usually underpaid and some-times reckon wedding fees as part of their regular income, and sextons may be put to quite a lot of extra work before and after a wedding. Commercial florists will of course charge their own fees.

No church ordinarily should make a charge for the use of the building by its own people, although churches which at-tract large numbers of weddings from outside their own membership sometimes do so. These matters should be worked out well in advance so that the wedding itself may be as its chief participants, the bride and the groom, will wish to remember it, and so that when the day comes they may be free to think of its real meaning.

4 · What Makes It Christian?

MONOGAMOUS MARRIAGE IS THE JOINING OF ONE MAN AND one woman by their free consent and, presumably, for life. But this contract can take place in a number of religious settings and contexts, or it can be strictly a civil transaction in the presence of a judge or a justice of the peace. There is no difference in the legality of the contract in any of these cases; but there is a difference in the nature and degree of responsibility assumed and there is a difference in the resources the couple may draw upon to strengthen and guide their marriage. None the less the question is a fair one: What makes it Christian?

In a real sense there is no such thing as "Christian marriage" as a thing in itself. The state usually so described is a marriage of two Christians to one another. That which makes such a union a Christian one is the same faith and practice which makes a Christian out of any man or woman. This is contrary to the popular notion that a marriage is a Christian one because it takes place in a Christian church building or is performed by a Christian minister. A Christian marriage could be contracted before a justice of the peace, if it were so intended and lived out, and doubtless this has happened. The heart of the matter is the nature and implications of the contract and the *intention* of the man and woman who enter into it.

First, let us look at it in a wide view, then narrow it down to some of the personal implications. The history of marriage shows many variations in form and structure. However in any and all of these it appears to be a response to our need for companionship, for love, for completion and, in a larger context, a response to our need for a stable society. Christians would say that marriage was provided by God in the natural order for these reasons. An anthropologist might observe that in the long development of life on this earth there emerged finally among the higher mammals male and female species which came to be known as human beings, and therefore the possibility of human community and communities. A Christian anthropologist would agree, but might add that he believes this process to be presided over by God the Maker of all things, to be in fact God's will.

The Doctrine of Creation

No one can consider the theology, the God-relationship, of Christian marriage without considering the doctrine of creation. God made everything that is, and declared it good. But there has been a Fall. We have only to look within ourselves to discover that we are not naturally good. No matter how much we try to make a good impression—sometimes to the extent of fooling even ourselves pretty thoroughly, because we agree to be fooled—we know that we are not good. We know that our motives are always mixed, that our first love is always ourselves. We may use different words to describe the fact that we live in a fallen world, but we know about the fact. Christians know that they live in a fallen world; they also know that it is a world to which the possibility of restoration is offered. Christians know that, since marriage is a part of the order of creation ordained by God, it, too, participates in the Fall no less than other institutions. This means three things: first, that by nature alone we cannot fulfill our obligations as marriage partners; secondly, that marriage requires and is subject to restoration; and, thirdly, that Christian marriage is essentially a sacramental relationship. The first of these truths gives the lie to the adequacy of the romantic dream. The second indicates the necessity and the actuality of a redeemer who knows all about us and our helplessness, and who involves himself compassionately with us where we are. Thirdly, the sacramental relationship means that this man and this woman represent nothing less than the grace of God to each other.

The biblical mythology describing the making of the world and of man is of course the creation story in *Genesis*. Mythology is not untruth; it is a way of speaking the truth in symbols—such as universal man and universal woman—when that is the only way or the best way in which to do it. We have already spent some time pointing out the romantic myth presupposed by our soap-opera approach to marriage. Thoughtful people have remarked upon the myth of the happy savage presupposed by the Kinsey reports. The biblical myth of creation means, among other things, that there is a responsible relationship between man and his creator and, therefore, between man and man or man and woman. The myths by which we live condition our judgment and our choices much more than we know or like to admit.

The *Genesis* story tells us that God, after making the physical world, made man and woman with equality and at the same time. "And God said, Let us make man in our own image, after our likeness . . . So God created man in his own image . . . male and female created he them." (*Genesis* 1:26,27) This is a later passage than the "rib" one and it was from this that Jesus quoted, even though he lived in a culture (as did these writers) in which women were regarded legally as property.

Some sense and a lot of nonsense has been written about the superiority of men to women. For many centuries in the East women have been chattels and in some places they still are; while in the Western world women were long regarded as the "weaker sex," to be admired, protected, and treated generally as second-class citizens. Recently the opposite line has been defended, and by men as well as women. It is pointed out that women are stronger (subject to fewer diseases, live longer), that they are emotionally more stable (fewer suicides, fewer mental patients), that they can do a number of jobs better and faster (handling small parts in the airplane industry, for instance). These and other similar observations may well be true at any given time, and many of them reflect cultural changes in our society. They are certainly interesting but I doubt that they are basic to our present inquiry. What is basic is the primary observation by this writer in *Genesis* that God created human beings in two orders, to love, fulfill, and complete each other. We shall think more about some of the cultural differences and tensions in a later chapter.

The average couple about to get married think of themselves and their marriage as different. They know, theoretically at least, some of the folklore about dangers and pitfalls and necessary adjustments, but they find these things difficult to apply to their own situation. Ordinarily this is not a feeling of self-conscious arrogance so much as it is a gratitude for good luck. And the state of being in love leads one to discover goodness, beauty, wisdom, and assorted perfections in the person of the beloved. This is not "bad"; in fact it is inevitable. But it is inadequate. As a starting place for natural man it is a part of the order of nature, but without some suspicion of the fall of man, it might be compared to driving an automobile on a busy street with one's eyes tightly closed.

Similarly, it is a part of our human nature to regard ourselves as adequate persons. Each of us begins life as the center of attraction. Each secretly considers himself his own authority in judging other people. We excuse ourselves elaborately and carefully when we are found in the wrong. As time goes on practice makes us more skillful at concealing our faults and in displaying our virtues winningly, even "modestly"! The truth-telling of judgment usually comes quietly. I can recall vividly a small incident from a number of years ago when I was torpedoed quite unintentionally by a soft-spoken little girl, my middle child, who was then about five years old. All washed and ready for bed she came downstairs to say goodnight. I was on my knees looking for a book on the bottom shelf when she walked softly toward me on little flannel feet, put her hand lightly on my shoulder and said with the deliberateness of childhood, "I have come to the conclusion that you are a very good man." What a blow! What a shattering, devastating blow! The naked exposure of trust. One feels like disappearing through the floor saying, "My darling child, I wish to God I were." At such a moment the cheapness of one's life is painfully clear. The easy lies, the pretenses, the strut and pose, the fear of the truth, the slipperiness, all are as if brilliantly lighted on a stage. We do not look at such a scene very long, it is too unsettling. Neither do we forget it entirely. And many of us are willing to admit at least some of the truth about us to ourselves, though we might defend ourselves with some vigor if another person said the same things about us. Gradually, as we begin to grow up a little, we begin to discover some lacks in our sufficiency, some deep needs in our supposed adequacy. We may even, in our hard-won little store of wisdom, come to the point where we know that we are fools and that if anyone loves us at all it is a gift and not a deserving. We may come to the moment of truth when we realize that the essence of the human situation is that no man can deliver himself or justify himself or forgive himself. If we are to be delivered, justified, or forgiven, it will have to be by someone other than ourselves, someone who is ready, willing, and able. This is the heart of the Christian religion, that God who made the world also redeemed it; that God entered his own creation in the person of Christ the Lord and bought it back by taking our place; that Christ, the adequate man, the free man, restores us to adequacy and to freedom in himself.

No Power of Ourselves

The central truth of a Christian marriage is the fact of Christ, God's redeeming action in the human situation. Whatever our bright hopes and good intentions, we are simply unable to cope with our "fallenness" by ourselves. Our self-love is too strong, and too subtle. One of our contemporary poets says, "Everywhere I go, I go too, and spoil everything." The "fall of man" occurs in every marriage; in a sense the marriage is not real until after that event. To some extent we all marry "ideal" mates, partly as an exten-

sion of our own egos. The problem is that of accepting ourselves the way we are before we can accept another person
the way he or she is. And here is the fact of Christ, the man-
in-God who comes, by his self-offering, to heal the breach between man and God, between man and man, and between a
man and himself.

One of the great watersheds of Christian thought stands
out clearly here. One side of this divide pretends that there
is some course of action, some way of keeping a set of rules,
by which a man can make himself morally desirable to God,
can achieve righteousness, can in a sense save himself. This
point of view turns up under various names through the centuries, and it dies hard. It is a vanity and a blasphemy. No
man can make himself pleasing to God by doing things or
by not doing things. The good news is much better than
that. The Christian faith is an act of trust in a person who
loves us, saves us, dies for us, not because we are good but
because *he* is. The motive for God's action, if we can use
such a word, is God's nature, nothing else. We cannot earn
God's love (or anyone's) or deserve it. It is a gift. It is *the*
gift.

It is Christ who accepts us the way we are—to the extent
of dying in our place, not only in some far-off geography of
time but right now, and again and again. Does this sound
strange and unreal? Perhaps an illustration may help.
There was once a young couple who had been married three
years and had one child. We had talked together about
Christian marriage and I had officiated at their wedding but
had seen them only once or twice since then because they
had moved to another community. Then some time later
they stopped in on their vacation to tell me this story. It
seems that they had gone through the usual period of adjust-

ment, but for some unknown and annoying reason the little misunderstandings never seemed to get really settled. So they went along. The child was born; and for a while their lives were sufficiently different so that the pattern was broken. But after a while they seemed to settle back into it again with steadily recurring little flare-ups. Then came the night of the big row. There had been many little ones—too many—but this one was different. They took up battle stations and threw heavy stuff which they meant to land. When the smoke of this verbal battle had cleared somewhat the young wife went silently upstairs. She sat on the bed and thought. She took her time getting ready for bed, hoping her husband would come up and that somehow life would go on. He did not. She waited a bit longer, then when she could not stand it another minute she walked quietly half way down the stairs to see what was going on. The young man was writing something on his lap. The rest of the story is in their own words.

"Are you coming to bed, John?"

"When I get damned good and ready."

(*A pause.*)

"What are you doing, John?"

"I don't think it would make you very happy if I told you."

(*Then, in that tone.*) "John, I am asking you. What are you doing?"

"OK, you asked me. I'm making a list of the things you do that gripe the hell out of me!"

The girl came down the rest of the stairs to confront her husband, her eyes round with astonishment. "Why John, do you have a list too?"

Then after a long moment the miracle began to happen. She stood in front of her husband, looking down at him, knowing something important for the first time. "John," she said in quite a different voice, "I have just discovered something."

"Yeah? What is it?" said John, not too interested.

"I have discovered," she said evenly and with just a touch of amazement, "that I like you the way you are."

Very slowly John raised his head and looked deeply into his wife's eyes to see if she was telling the truth. She was. All the anger went out of him, all the annoyance, all the hurt. He stood up and took her in his arms dropping his list behind her on the floor. Then he carried her upstairs.

What they had come to say was that that was the night they got married. They had been living in the same house for three years and they had produced a child, but that was the night of the real marriage, the real acceptance.

As one begins to accept the miracle of his acceptance in Christ (often by way of another quite ordinary person), even so he begins to see himself in scale, perhaps even with a little humor. Then one begins to be able really to "meet" another person, one's husband or wife for instance, to whom one may have been married for years. The power to do this, whether we know it or not, is the power of God the creator. He who makes new—revealed, demonstrated, made available in Christ the Lord.

To be quite practical, this means at least two things. It means that there is a Christian community. Just as this marriage is important to the civil society of which it is a part, so it is important to the Christian society of which it is a part, the Church, the Body of Christ. But with a difference. The interest of the state is merely horizontal, here and now, while the Church is interested in this man and this woman not only now but for all eternity. When the newly married couple become working members of the Church in the place where they have gone to live, they join themselves not only to their fellow saints and sinners in that place but to all Christians in every place, and to the whole company of heaven. One might say that this is the newly married couple's expression of their baptism. This is the frame, this local worshipping community, in which their hopes and plans will be worked out, their mistakes made, their turning points reached. Here they will be supported in love by the brethren, here they will receive the bread of life.

This means, secondly, that because of the compassion of the Lord supporting them they can afford to be wrong. Otherwise it is too costly. It is one thing to be proved wrong, damaging to the pride and frequently resulting in hardness of heart. It is quite another thing to be willing to be wrong, knowing that one is loved. To put it another way, a Christian can afford to be forgiving because he knows himself to be forgiven. This is why the parties to this marriage represent nothing less than the grace of God to each other. It is still an adventure, a life to be lived without guarantees, but it is a good companionship in all of the departments of living, and one based on a deeper companionship in the Lord.

Christian marriage is an actuality as well as an aspiration. It happens. And when it does happen it is not an accident; it is a living relationship, creative and free, built consciously on a common love and worship of God as He reveals Himself in Jesus Christ and in the people of God. It is the union of two souls and bodies who can dare to be joyful because they accept the fact of their redemption; who can endure loneliness and fear for a season because they know that the risen Christ is at one with their humanity; who can live in forbearance and good humor and can die in peace because they know that there is a God who made them and holds them and is their life.

When this man and this woman stand before the altar and say I John take thee Mary, it is as if each of them were holding his life in his hands, saying, You take it; I want you to have it, all of it, forever, and with no strings attached. Later on both of these persons will be able to give more than they can at this moment but my concern now is with what is received. It is a joy, a wonder, a trust, a responsibility. A life relationship with an unknown future has been committed to another person, willingly and gladly. And that is what has been received.

The Christian . . . Is in Love

We have thought about the words of the betrothal promises: love, comfort, honor, keep. We might consider briefly the added meaning of these words for Christians. When the Church uses the word love in the marriage service, the image produced in the minds of the assembled people is more likely to be shaped by Hollywood than by St. Paul's hymn to love which we know as chapter thirteen in his first letter to the Corinthians. St. Paul knew nothing of chapters and verses when he was pouring out his heart to the young church at Corinth, but he did know how his whole world had been seized and turned around by a loving God, and he had to say so. In phrase after phrase, in one of the great pieces of writing in any language, this God-filled man describes what love *does*, but he does not once mention how love *feels*. "Charity suffereth long, and is kind," says the familiar version. "Love has good manners," translates a contemporary version. Still another says, "There is nothing love cannot face." This is love as a motive, not a feeling. It is grown-up love which is not at the mercy of a whim or a mood. It is—and this is the real meaning—a reflection however imperfect of the love of God for us, which is clean, straight, complete good will. God loves us not because we are so lovable but because He is so loving. When one's husband or wife is silly or angry or sulky or coldly distant, it takes more loving and more strength to be kind, to have good manners, or to face it, than does the rare romantic moment when all the world is golden and all one's geese are swans. We know about this tough, generous, lasting sort of love (which makes romantic love possible as a by-product) because God shows it to us in the person of Jesus Christ. It is difficult for us to grasp the idea of unconditional love because our love is so conditioned by another person's response. But God loves us without condition, without bargaining, without "let or hindrance." The Christian, by definition, is "in love." Christian marriage is one of the settings in which this love can be lived out, in bright days and in dark ones.

So with the other words. Each has a Christian dimension, a depth, which the world at large does not know. God himself is called the Comforter, the Holy Spirit who strengthens and encourages. God honors every child of his with respect for that person as an end in himself, his essential dignity as a man. And God keeps us in all our ways in this life and for eternity. He will never let us go. In the state of Christian marriage the generosity, the steadiness, the givenness of God's attitude toward us is reflected back to God, as far as we are able, and in him to the man or woman we love.

When in the marriage vows we commit ourselves to one another "in the sight of God and in the face of this company," and receive each other's self-offering, we make ourselves responsible for the other's growing room. Many people will wish the newly married couple happiness. It is a good wish and an easy word but it is not a very tall word. There will be many times without happiness but not necessarily without love. In fact it is often in the unhappy times that love is really known for what it is. The marriage commitment is deep and lasting. These persons are promising to help each other to grow up into the best person that each can be—free, honest, loving, whole. And both the giving and the receiving are done as a reflection of the gracious way in which God gives himself to us and receives us.

The preface to the Solemnization of Matrimony in The Book of Common Prayer has an interesting phrase to describe Christian marriage: "signifying unto us the mystical union which is betwixt Christ and his Church," an allusion to the part of the fifth chapter of the *Epistle to The Ephesians* (5:20-33) which is the appointed Epistle when the Holy Communion is celebrated at a marriage. Mystical union is the Church's way of saying that more is involved here for Christians, both in responsibility and resource, than in a civil contract or a social convention. Any individual Christian is "in Christ"; this is his new being. In the Holy Communion we pray that we may "dwell in him, and he in us." Here in this sacrament of Christian union these two Christians commit themselves to God and to each other in Christ. There is a sacred welding of this man and this woman in which God is involved.

In a Christian marriage the added dimension is our knowledge of God's compassionate involvement in the person of Christ in the everyday stuff of living and dying and being born again which happens many times. Whatever loneliness or fear or frustration we may feel—and we do—God knows about it and shares it. Martin Buber says that love is the revealing by two people of the "thou" to one another. This is possible because God has revealed himself in a person, a life, which we can share. God reveals himself constantly through the people of God. We know about him in Christ but he touches us by way of the flesh and blood people with whom we live. So in the circle of a Christian marriage these two people of God may reveal his love to each other more fully and freely than in any other human relationship.

Note:

A word needs to be said, I think, about marriages which are not Christian in any formal or technical sense but which seem to be good ones none the less. It would be dishonest to pretend that they do not exist, though honest enough to wonder how such people meet tragedy. But a marriage can be godly without the parties to it knowing the source of its goodness, just as many of the aspects of what we call, somewhat loosely, "Western Civilization" are based upon a Christian knowledge of God and man and the relationship between them. We should be grateful when we see a good and creative marriage outside of the Christian community. God is not limited by our limitations or by our understanding of his workings or by the boundaries of the Church. At the same time we are responsible for what we know and believe. We are grateful for our knowledge of the resources within the Christian family because we know that we need all the help we can get, and we are eager that these resources may be known by our friends.

5 · *The Practice of Religion*

"The function of Christian marriage is that two people may become, *in fact*, one, for the purpose of witnessing to the Christian life and of bringing up children in that life. It is to create a union between two people which will be characterized by such mutual interdependence that it will be, by definition, indissoluble. The nature of Christian marriage is nothing less than salvation. 'A type of the mystical union between Christ and His Church' is more than just a phrase —the Christian married life carries within it all of the marks of the redemptive life of our Lord. The married person lives a life of atonement and self-oblation, and the extent to which he destroys self will be the measure of the success of his marriage. The sacrifices of Christ for his Church are made again and again by mate for mate. In the marriage relationship the 'matter' of the sacrament of marriage is found in a life together which is redeemed and redeeming."

These words were written a few years ago by a former student of mine, the Reverend Richard E. Byfield, and will serve as a transition from our concern of the last chapter with the nature of Christian marriage to the concern of the present one with how we practice it.

The Third Guest

The burden of our thought thus far is that God has provided the institution of marriage which is now a part of the fallen creation, but subject to restoration and wholeness in Christ. God never leads us by a lie. He will always tell the truth about us, sometimes by way of a profound silence, but he is always gracious, always courteous. He waits to be invited into our lives as a welcome guest. Our lives are kept open by courtesies. In a deep sense our wife or our husband is our guest for life. This is our most important person, the one we have asked to share our bread and our tears, our nights and our days. So as we would prepare our heart and our home for a beloved guest, so should we prepare for every home-coming of this man, this woman.

In most marriages that I know anything about this attitude is not usually the most noticeable after the first bloom. Not that one sets out to be discourteous; one just forgets to notice or takes for granted or assumes. After a while we tend to save our pretty looks for strangers. We need the third guest. We need the God who made us and who loves us more than we love each other, more even than we love ourselves. We shall always have God's good will; we need to invite his company. If it is true, as Christians believe, that God is our primary and sustaining lover, then the most intelligent thing we could do would be to invite him into our marriage. How does one do this? Speaking generally, there are two ways: public and private, outside and inside.

In the Body of the Church

Let us think first of the public occasion and practice, then of the private. The marriage service is a public one because it is important to the public. No couple can be joined in marriage without at least two witnesses who are required to sign documents stating that they heard the words spoken. The Church feels this way too; a marriage is an act of the Church as well as an act of these individuals. Hopefully, these persons have been brought up in the household of faith, learning by living as well as by precept the nature of that faith and life. Now they come as members of the Church's household, the body of Christ in the world, to start a new life together with the Church's blessing and with the prayers of the Church family. In a way that we shall explore further, this marriage may be thought of as a little church, a small exhibit of the whole Christian society in which these people minister to each other, to their children, relatives and friends, in the name of the Lord. My former student says, "nothing less than salvation." Salvation is safeness, the safeness of being loved, sustained, held. This is what we receive from the Lord and what as members of his body, the Church, we offer to one another.

So it seems right that the wedding of two Christians should take place in the body of the church with the congregation assembled in the customary place of worship. The introduction (rubric) to the marriage service in The Book of Common Prayer says, "At the day and time appointed for Solemnization of Matrimony, the Persons to be married shall come into the body of the Church, or shall be ready in some proper house, with their friends and neighbours . . ." This direction has an interesting history. In English practice all Church marriages must take place in church unless conditions are so extraordinary as to justify a special dispensation called Archbishop's License. (For example, the fact that one of the parties to the marriage is bedridden.) Such was the practice when the Church of England first came to this country. In Colonial times, however, church marriages were often impossible because of the lack of churches; so that by the time the first American Prayer Book was published in 1790 the phrase "some proper house" was added out of practicality.

In our times the matter turns upon appropriateness. People sometimes want to be married at home because it is so "homey," or in the garden for romantic reasons, or in a hotel ballroom so that the picture-taking and the reception can begin at once and without transportation problems. There was a time not very long ago, one hopes now happily outgrown, when otherwise sensible people got married in submarines, airplanes, swimming pools, and subways.

Church people will wish to be married in church primarily because it is "home" for the faith community of which they are members. Here is the familiar scene, warm in the mind from many visits for many reasons. Here the important steps in one's own religious life were taken. Here one has grown up with his own family in the larger family of the gathered community. Here one has fought some of his own battles in the silence of his own prayers; here one has thought some of the thoughts that will stay with him always. Here one has been a part of the witnessing, praying congregation at the time of other people's marriages. And even though we have become a nation on wheels, the Church is the Church wherever one finds it. It is still "home" though it may be at the other side of the country, or of the world, from one's native heath.

Apart from the appropriateness of a wedding in church, it is much easier to manage. Whether a small wedding in a chapel, or one with many participants in a much larger place, the business of entrances and exits, the ability of the people to participate by seeing what is going on, the dignity of the whole proceeding—all are done better in church. There is something about the determined playing of the wedding march on the living-room piano, with a nervous glance over the shoulder to see if the timing is right, which smacks of the amateur theatrical.

Even small marriages need to have rehearsals so that people will know their parts and the event go off smoothly. And it is a help on the wedding day itself to be able to put one's whole mind (or as much of it as possible) on the real meaning of the occasion. When the moment finally comes, it is a solemn one. The bridegroom looks down the aisle to see a vision appear on her father's arm and wonders if he will be able to say anything at all. He will be comforted if he has already practiced his lines. Such simple things as knowing where to stand and when to move from one place to another can free the whole wedding party to make their best contribution to an occasion they will remember for years to come.

Documents

Some of the documents can be filled out at the time of the rehearsal, without the clergyman's signature of course, further freeing the day itself from these formalities. The number of necessary papers will differ slightly from state to state, but there will always be the marriage license and the parish register. In the Episcopal Church the bride and groom are required to sign a Declaration of Intention, giving their assent to the Church's understanding of the nature and purpose of Christian marriage. The words are good ones and will bear quoting: "We, A.B. and C.D. desiring to receive the blessing of Holy Matrimony in the Church, do solemnly declare that we hold marriage to be a lifelong union of husband and wife as it is set forth in the Form of Solemnization of Holy Matrimony in The Book of Common Prayer. We believe it is for the purpose of mutual fellowship, encouragement, and understanding, for the procreation (if it may be) of children, and their physical and spiritual nurture, for the safeguarding and benefit of society. And we do engage ourselves, so far as in us lies, to make our utmost effort to establish this relationship and to seek God's help thereto." It is the custom in many places for the newly married couple to be presented with the marriage service, in booklet form, which was actually used at their wedding. It is a convenient and attractive form in which to keep the marriage lines and one which can be reread from time to time.

The Holy Communion

It is most appropriate that the Holy Communion be celebrated in connection with the marriage, and for this purpose a proper Collect, Epistle, and Gospel are provided in the Prayer Book. There are two ways to do this. The bride and groom, and any members of the wedding party or the family whom they invite, may come together at some agreeable time on the morning of the wedding day for a nuptial celebration. It is a meaningful occasion for members of the household of faith to gather quietly in the presence of the

Lord for the first step in the new life together of this man and this woman on their day. There is also the advantage of a familiar act, and one of which they know some of the significance.

The other way is to combine the marriage service and the Holy Communion. There are variations in practice, but the general procedure is for the betrothal to take place after the wedding march (if any), at the foot of the chancel steps, followed by the movement of the wedding party to the altar rail, as usual, for the completion of the marriage ceremony. Then follows the service of Holy Communion with the newly married couple and their attendants kneeling at the altar rail and being the first to make their communions. Many feel that this liturgical practice is the best witness that the Church can make to what it believes about Christian marriage. Sometimes the bride and groom participate in bringing to the altar the vessels and the bread and wine to be used in the service. There is no reason why the marriage service cannot be used in connection with the regular parish eucharist, together with a sermon on the nature of Christian marriage. A reception in the parish hall after such a wedding may well contain an element which many wedding receptions lack.

Newly married people enjoy celebrating "anniversaries" —a week, a month, six months today! There is no better way to celebrate these glad days than to meet again at the altar—the family table—where this marriage began, and to offer in the Holy Communion one's hopes and plans and dreams. The Lord who "adorned and beautified with his presence and first miracle that he wrought (at the wedding) in Cana of Galilee," will understand and bless this man and this woman in their needs. And as the days and years roll on they will come again and again, later with their children, to this place of refuge and strength.

The Church Which Is in Thy House

After the festivities are over and the couple have come to live in their own place, wherever it may be, they are a new unit, a husband and wife, a potential family. It is as such that they attend the local church and become a part of its life. They may do so as regular worshippers, returning prayer and praise for their blessings, drawing strength for their needs. Or, added to that, they may become involved in the program of the parish, finding expression for their abilities and interests. It is no news that this can be over-done. Someone has observed that there is no substitute for religion like church work! It seems beyond argument that many young couples, especially in suburbia, do become en-grossed in the busy-work aspects of church organization, to the detriment of their own religious life and that of the local church. There will always be real needs to be met and gen-uine calls for help to be heard and heeded; but the deep need of this new family is quietly to become itself. It is easy for us to confuse our priorities, to make a sort of religion of being busy about the church building or its concerns, and in doing so to lose sight of the real reason for its being there—to be a tabernacle in the wilderness for souls on pilgrimage. It is easy for the Church to become indistinguishable from the other exhibits of our culture which surround it. There is a necessary relationship here or the Church cannot speak to the world around it; but by the same token the world can speak to the Church so effectively that its values become those of the world. It may be that this new couple already know some of these things, not only for their own good but for the benefit of some of their contemporaries as well.

Apart from the public expression of their life as a new unit of society, a new family with duties and responsibilities and problems and joys, these people have a private life which is their own. Whatever they do in the world will be a reflection of who they are as individuals and what their private world together is like. This private life will have many facets, but for Christians an important part of it will be religious. Reference has been made to "the church which is in thy house," an expression used by St. Paul in one of his letters. This is the heart of the matter. The larger church is made up of individuals and of "house-churches" where the practice of religion from day to day shapes the life and defines the purposes of the people of God. One has a house or an apartment with a street and a number where the life goes on—bed and board, gaieties and griefs, special events and daily humdrum. But within those walls, for people who have stood before an altar and made their promises in the sight of God, is a church, a small but important worshipping community. There is an exchange between the life of the larger church and the life of the church at home; each needs and complements the other.

With every newly married couple there will be some variation in the practice of private prayer. One may have stopped saying his prayers after he left "mother's knee," and in his young adulthood have rightly outgrown that practice without ever having discovered anything better to put in its place. Some do not have even that much to remember. Others will have grown in their understanding and practice of the life of prayer as they have grown in other ways. Almost everyone will have prayed, even though rarely, in his own emergencies. The average couple will have had some prayer discipline thrust upon them when very young, and some will have persisted; but for most the practice of private prayer will not seem a necessity.

Here, beginning with the day of the wedding, is an opportunity to grow together, and to grow up together, in a way which no other can supply. Whatever their practice may have been as individuals, when these two people kneel down together the first night after they have married each other, they are beginning an adventure of faith which may become the most important thing in their common life. On the first night they might well say the Lord's Prayer together aloud, then silently say whatever is on their minds. As a man and woman in love they will ask God's blessing on their marriage. Each will be wordlessly thankful for his remarkable good fortune in having married this wonderful person who might so easily have married someone else. One can think of many reasons for loving his new wife, or her new husband; the reasons are so obvious. But one can think of no reason why this person among millions should love him, or her, except that it is so. It seems a miracle. A silent prayer may be breathed that one may become worthy of this person who thinks one is better than he is. This is the way God treats us, as if we were better than we are, and it is our hope of becoming so.

And so the adventure of prayer begins in this household. It will go well at first because it *is* an adventure and a new way of sharing two lives. But if they persist they will come to a desert. Everyone who has ever tried to pray regularly knows about that desert. It is wide and dry. Nothing grows there. The whole business seems like meaningless motion and, if one were simply on his own, this might well be the end of the adventure. For many it has been. But now there is a difference, a double difference. First, one has a companion on the journey. There are two crossing the desert this time and they are walking together. They may remark upon the scenery, or lack of it, but neither is alone any more. The other difference is that the two are likely to move at different degrees of awareness at different times. So one, being dry and standing still, may be refreshed by the other's movement and discovery. And the discovery can be talked about. We sometimes act as if the practice of prayer were so personal that it could not be discussed in a normal way by normal people. Certainly it is true that private prayer is a personal encounter and that little can be said about it even if one were so minded. Certainly it is true that as one grows toward God even a very little, increasingly more of his life becomes a part of his religious life in a way difficult to describe. But it is also true that this married couple who wish to share with each other as much of their separate lives as they can, may find in the adventure of prayer together one of the deepest sources of their self-understanding and their understanding of one another.

People who live together closely are bound to have differences of opinion, not because they are those particular individuals but because they are human beings. Each of us has quirks that annoy, or habit patterns which seem obviously sensible to us but strange indeed to another. All of us have our bad days. On such occasions a small difference of opinion is liable to become suddenly much larger than it has any right to be. Tempers rise, hearts harden, words are spoken, doors slam, silence is thick and heavy. Who has not known such times to some degree? Sometimes they just get themselves over with. The wind goes down and the sea is calm again. Sometimes they persist and rankle, becoming fuel for future fires. Again, there are no guarantees; but if these same people were to say their prayers together that night because it was their custom, the likelihood of the continuance of the little storm would be greatly decreased. They would have met at a level so simple and open and honest that the difference of opinion which started the whole thing off would have disappeared—or at least it could be talked about. The third guest would have been invited.

Many troubles can be handled, if not "solved," if people have a place where they can meet and be themselves. A few years ago a young woman, married to an apprentice machinist, wrote me a letter illustrating this. Not long after the marriage, her husband lost his job because of a strike and was unable to find another. It was not long before their savings were used up and they had to leave their apartment. There was no place for them to go except the home of the bride's parents. Never an ideal situation, this one was complicated by the fact that the young wife's brother, who also lived at home, resented their moving in. They had never hit it off very well. Frequent references were made to the fact that, though he did not have the education of the other man, he *did* have a job. This went on for a number of weeks, at times narrowly missing actual battle, when a settlement was made in the strike situation and machinists were once again sought after. The girl wrote quite simply that she and her husband had agreed that their being able to move out with as little emotional damage as they had and to set up housekeeping on their own again was due to the fact that they said their prayers together at night. It was their shelter and their citadel. The troublesome brother could not scale the walls here, and from that safe place they could meet the next day's demands of job hunting and temper-keeping; they could even salvage occasional scraps of humor, knowing they were held.

Sometimes there are deep troubles. When the bride and groom drive away from the reception in a shower of rice and confetti, their future seems bright with promise. They are young, eager, attractive. They are also vulnerable. No one knows what lies in the path ahead; but none of us escapes being hurt, sometimes badly. More often than not we do not know about other people's serious trouble, since we all turn our best face to the world. The real question is, with what resources do we meet our problem when it comes? No person has more faith than he can summon in an emergency. No one can draw money from the bank which is not there in his name. If, day by day, this man and this woman have come quietly into the presence of God who knows our joys, our disappointments, and our sorrows, when the bad time comes they will have a known friend in whom to meet. The trouble will be just as bad; but there will be a way of absorbing it, as our hurts and hates are absorbed by a loving Lord.

It happens more often than not, when children in a family come to the point when it is good for them to begin to learn to pray, that they do so at "mother's knee" because there is no better place available. But how good for the child if he were to discover that the practice of prayer in his home was as natural as the other things that normally go on in homes; that his father and mother have been doing this for years as an important part of their life together. Such a child would not have to begin saying his prayers as if he were the only person in the world doing so; he would grow up in a household where prayers together were a normal part of a normal day. And as he and his brothers and sisters came along, they would be included in this family activity, and their special concerns and important events shared with those of their parents as conversation is shared at the table. It could be the parents' best gift to their children.

Casting our minds into the future, there will come a time when one of the partners in this marriage will be left alone, perhaps for some years. In a way, the better the marriage the greater the sense of loss. The passage of time does help, yet the loneliness is still there. So one prays to a loving God—remembering the good years, knowing that though our loved ones are absent from us, no one is absent from God.

It is never too late to learn to pray. A young lawyer friend of mine, married and the father of four lively children, told me once that in his opinion the "dark night of the soul" is not at three o'clock in the morning for a desert saint, but about five-thirty p.m. on the commuting train for home. A hard day at the office *versus* a hard day on the home front, each combatant waiting to tell his story first, to enlist the sympathy so rightly deserved. Bill says he learned to pray on that train, really pray, for the first time in his life—to hold his peace, to listen, to be open and loving. And so, from him, did his wife. No halos appeared and nothing was changed—no *thing*—but two people were.

Prayer goes on all the time; we do not initiate it, we join it. When we have stated times for our prayers together, not by the clock but by events such as bedtime or breakfast, we are more likely to say them. Then we begin to pray during the daily round and, eventually, our lives themselves become an offering.

6 · Sex

SEXUALITY IS THE GIFT OF GOD; NOT ONLY IN THE OBVIOUS
and the subtle ways in which men differ from women, not
only in the ability to produce more persons like themselves
but, more important than these, in the ability to meet one
another—fully, deeply, and truly to meet. In the Author-
ized Version of the Bible, the King James, the verb "to know"
is used to describe the act of sexual union. For example,
"And Cain knew his wife; and she conceived, and bore
Enoch." (*Genesis 4:17*) Many think that sex is the most
important single factor of our existence, and it well may be
so. Certainly it is one of the profound keys to the expression
of a personality or a culture. Paintings and sculptures of
the beautiful or the erotic, published photographs, novels,
plays and poems in which sexuality is explored and inter-
preted tell us a great deal of what people think about themselves and about life. Symbols of the beautiful and the sex-
ually desirable change from time to time and from place to
place; but all peoples create such symbols and defend them
and live by them. Basically, sex is life. Sex is mystery. Sex
is a reaching out for fulfillment because its essential nature
is incompleteness.

Love and Sex

We sometimes confuse the words love and sex, and in common speech we do not always distinguish clearly between sex and the act of sexual union. Perhaps some clarification may be possible here. All love is a response to being loved, ultimately by God. We have already thought about God's love for us as straight, unconditional good will, independent of anything we might do to deserve it or not deserve it. None of us can manage this except for short periods of time and under favorable circumstances. Whenever it does appear, God's love as revealed in Christ is the source and possibility of it. Any loving of this kind that we do is a pale and broken reflection of God's love for us. The words "I love you" rightly mean I care about you, about what happens to you, and I desire your good quite apart from whether or not I get anything out of it myself. In the exchange of the betrothal promises in the marriage service we do not say that we love this person (it is assumed that we do); but we promise to keep on doing so through thick and thin, and to the end of our lives. The married couple assume a godly responsibility for each other.

The primary meaning of the word sex is the simple description of maleness or femaleness. Sometimes it is used to mean sexuality and, even more confusing, it sometimes means the sexual act. Sexuality, among human beings, is a way of expressing love. The fact that men and women can complete each other, can become one flesh, is a fact of nature, but nature is a part of the givenness of God. Here in the mystery of sex is another window on the "mystical union," a type of our possible union with God. Many have remarked upon the similarity between religious and sexual symbols: loving, desiring, serving, belonging, offering, living for and in, for example. The meaning of sex is not primarily moral or biological but religious, because it has to do with meaning—my meaning, our meaning. My own masculinity is known in terms of the other's femininity, not only as function but as being.

The sex act can mean any number of things. It is a sort of barometer, an indicator, of whatever is intended. At its lowest level, the level of unadorned sensual gratification, it can mean nothing more than irresponsible sensation. A G.I. definition of the ideal girl friend will illustrate this: A beautiful, blond, deaf and dumb nymphomaniac who has no relatives and owns a liquor store. Our hero in the world of such a definition is the tough-talking, fist-swinging male familiar to the readers of a type of paperback thriller. He drinks bourbon by the case, consumes steaks by the dozen, and women fall for his rugged charm like tenpins in a bowling alley. This sort of tale is the fastest selling fiction in America, a fact which might argue that it represents the dream world of a considerable number of people. We call it escape literature and so it is, but it is interesting to observe the kind of world to which many choose to escape.

Some years ago when I was a pastor in a New England college town an incident occurred which produced a remark I have never forgotten. On a Monday morning an attractive college girl, one I knew quite well, came into my office sputtering with indignation. She had been at a party the night before with several other couples—the sort of party which seemed to be the order of the day right after the war when thousands of young men came back from battlefield to college campus with their fangs still showing. My student and her fellow dates had been "necked" almost to the point of no return when the party finally broke up. What she had to say, the remark that stuck in my mind, was that what she really objected to was being treated as a female occasion. She was far from being a prude; but she was impressed by the fact that her name did not matter, nor her future, nor anything, really, except that she was a female and within reach. She could have changed places with someone else in the dark and it would not have made any difference. There is a type of man who seems never to grow beyond this point. Any woman will do as long as she is warm, cuddly, and available.

Almost the worst that one can say about the institution of prostitution is that the encounter is meaningless. One buys a commodity, a certain amount of sensation and release of tension, and goes away. The two people never meet as people, as beings. They meet only as functions. The same can be said for nameless sexual promiscuity, the pursuit of sensation without responsibility. Perhaps the most dangerous words to learn in any language are "I love you." They are an easy gate to casual sexual satisfaction because everybody wants to believe that they are true. Thousands of sexual incidents have taken place, and will take place, because one hoped that this time the words might be true and the event have a meaning.

Much has been written about pre-marital sex experience. It is not my intention to rehearse that easily available data here except as it bears upon our general subject, the maturity of a Christian marriage. Any normally intelligent person at a time when objectivity is possible, and not at the moment of crisis, can understand that a sexual relationship which is nervous with fears—fears of discovery, pregnancy, possible disease, destructive emotional consequences—is not the best possible setting for full and free exchange. Engagements are broken for a variety of reasons, no matter how sure one feels at the time. There is also the matter of guilt, even though one may believe it to have been banished by some form of intellectual "flit." And there is the mysterious business of giving more of oneself than one meant to and not being able to get it back. No act performed is so irrevocable as a human relation. A part of one may belong to that person forever.

All of these are honest and ponderable considerations. It is only fair to say on the other side that good material washes and that genuine love is strong enough and generous enough to absorb anything. One does not have a right (love has no "rights") to ask about the other person's past. Either you love this man or this woman with all your heart and from this moment on, or you do not. If you do, then nothing else matters. In such a case the quality of freedom will probably be such that anything whatever can be discussed freely and openly. So much the better. But if one loves he does not pry; he waits for the gift of confidence, and he gives it.

The real question is, what do I want? What do *we* want? If this marriage is the beginning of a new life together, approved by society and blessed by God, then the couple may decide for their own reasons, including religious ones, that they will wait to begin this new life together as completely as possible. Americans tend to make a fetish of the perfect sex act—a cruel piece of make-believe which causes a lot of unnecessary mental and emotional suffering. Occasionally there comes such an experience of almost unbelievable height and depth and satisfaction; but it is impossible to predict, except to say that it is unlikely to happen in the early stages of a marriage, and even less so before marriage. Too much has to be learned and felt and known. The real difference is between what it is and what it means. Here in the security of marriage is the real meeting place for this man and this woman, for love is the enemy of haste. Here they have time and privacy, approval and blessing, and each other. Here they come to each other gladly and thankfully in the knitting together of two, free, whole, human beings— bodies, spirits, minds—willing to fulfill and to be fulfilled. This miracle of meeting gathers up all the tapestry of their common life: their worries and their unexpected joys, their private jokes that are no one else's business, their hopes and plans and dreams. And the secret joining says, "This is us, this is ourselves, our self." It expresses sacramentally the meaning of the marriage and at the same time it is the means for more meaning.

In his book, *The Divine Realm*, Eugueny Lampert, a contemporary theologian, has this to say about the meaning of the union of man and woman in one flesh:

"There is here enacted above all the ultimate outgoing of man from himself into the waiting depths of being. He descends and plunges into the word 'beneath' and 'above' himself, into the breath of the morning of creation, into the dawn of being. It is the moment, when in awestruck trembling life transcends its limits. The womb of the world is pierced, and through the narrow crater of a tremendous act are, as it were, perceived a new 'beneath' and a new 'above,' a 'new earth' and a 'new heaven.' It is the mystery where heaven sheds itself on man, and man yields to heaven; the mystery of the breaking down of all the limits and limitations

of human life and isolated human existence, of the petrified
and stagnant flesh of man. It is the mystery of a sudden
merging and union into a single, indivisible being of flesh
and spirit, of heaven and earth, of human and divine love.
The divine spirit touches human flesh, since it is transparent
to Him in its primeval depth, and indeed receives Him in
the burning moment of erotic ecstasy. We are witnessing to
a true sacrament: the Spirit of God invades the cosmic element, without ceasing to be the Spirit, and the flesh widens
into the transcendence of the Spirit, without ceasing to be
flesh." *

In married love one of the best fruits of the sexual union
comes afterward when, fulfilled and happy in having completed each other, the couple are themselves. There is no
place to go, they have already arrived. This act depends for
its meaning and satisfaction on that which it conveys and
speaks for. Even in marriage it is possible for it to be an act
of indifference, or of hostility. The act, as such, has little or
no meaning in itself. Everything depends on what it says.
It can say convenience or habit or duty. It can also say "I
love you" better than any words. Sex is the communication
of all that lies too deep for words and yet that somehow must
be told.

Soul and Body

Basic to any understanding of Christian marriage is the
Christian concept of the body. God made it, and whatever
God makes is good. The body is real, not ideal. The end of

* Euguney Lampert, *The Divine Realm* (London: Faber and Faber,
1943), pp. 97,98.

the body, in Christian teaching, is not to melt into nothingness, or to deny itself, but to be fulfilled in the fulness of Christ who became man for our salvation and who in his resurrected flesh is the Son of God. In the New Testament Christ himself is called "the saviour of the body" (*Ephesians* 5:23). Our bodies are the instruments of our self-expression just as the Church is in the New Testament repeatedly described as the Body of Christ, the instrument of his saving activity in the world. Man is not a soul but a soul and body, a self. The only experience we can have of ourselves and of others is through the body. Archbishop Temple once called Christianity the most materialistic of all religions. That is to say it is sacramental, meaning speaking through matter. It does not deny matter; the spirit speaks through the body. So any Christian marriage, lived out by ordinary Christians, is a unity of matter and spirit, body and soul, and the unity of God with his creation is symbolized by the union of their two bodies and spirits.

The phrase "the act of love" is both expressive and misleading. It is expressive in that it attempts to describe the motivation of the act, the reason for the coming together. It is misleading in that it tends to isolate the act from that which precedes and follows it. Love, like truth, is all of a piece and is expressed in many ways. Few, if any, of these expressions are as intense as the act of sexual union, but this is the chief difference. A series of sexual acts, however satisfying in themselves, would not make a marriage. The common life of this couple in all of its aspects, public and private, are or can be acts of love. When man and wife minister to one another with tenderness and compassion, when they respect each other's privacy, when they hold their tongues instead of saying something destructive, however true, these are acts of love. And so, too, are their blessed times of nonsense and hilarity. All of it goes into the weaving together of two lives into one life; and when they meet deeply in their bodies and spirits all these things are spoken for and cemented.

When two young people fall in love everything is different. The world seems to be newly washed and sparkling. It has a morning face. It is an agreeable place. The sky is more blue, the grass is greener. Things scarcely noticed before take on a startling clarity. People exhibit postures of good will which recently would have gone unnoticed or have seemed impossible. It is a dream of fairness and goodness and generosity. And so it is. Later on, when dream and reality are intermingled, it is even better. When two people —no longer that boy and that girl—are successfully in love their two worlds and their common world are enriched. They know a vigor and a strength impossible to them separately. They walk with a lighter step, they think more clearly, they sleep more soundly, and they can do more than they dreamed possible. Their sexual intimacy—instead of being the dead end of desire, the sightless and temporary possession of another body—becomes a spring of energy and joy. Their love grows because it has something to grow upon and to grow with. It is not limited by the memory of a romantic event impossible to recapture. It is not throttled by sentimentalism. It is rooted and grounded in a love which is greater than theirs and which sustains it.

A poet-housewife friend of mine writes:

"Curious, how the antithetical views of the way of Affirmation and the Puritan anti-sensualism should both move towards an appreciation of morality—for such different reasons! The virtue of chastity (properly understood as not identical at all with continence)—the Puritan view is that chastity is great because the flesh is itself evil and needs discipline; because the horror of the body makes chastity a way of escaping from the corruption of sex (and therefore the decaying, ageing body). Yet the Incarnational view of chastity is that it is great because the body is so precious and sexuality so holy and stupendous (and powerful!) a gift that it should be truly fulfilled in that whole human-to-human relationship which is, or ought to be, marriage. Chastity as not an escape but as an ordering toward fulfillment—

How intense—yet not tense—is ordered sexuality, springing from, being an expression of, as well as a means of the relation of love! Making love—how profoundly true is this phrase, not a 'euphemism' at all, but a realistic description. And along with this majestic and gracious gift of sexuality, to have also the growing, quiet grace of simple easy sensuality. Touch expressing affection, warmth, communicating this and so much unspeakable—touch out of abundance and satisfaction, not out of need or desire, yet free to express desire also. In view of this, chastity is a simple corollary, which springs naturally from the understanding of the relationship.

The freedom to be and to act—even to discover, all over again, that there is not, natively, the division between *being* and *acting*—is the gift of love, of loving and being loved at the same time."

The Two Worlds of Marriage

Marriage is not an end in itself, but a means for the expression of love. Women are usually better off than men in expressing their love, since it is more diffused. For a man love, or loving, is more likely to be an event joined somewhat tenuously to other events. He rises from the marriage bed with worlds to conquer or rolls over and goes to sleep; but in either case the loving moment is a thing in the past. He may feel tender and grateful toward his wife and lover, he may look forward to other such ecstatic moments, but the loving events are like beads on a string. Not so the woman. In her case the loving encounter is a spring of well-being, a feeling-tone which conditions everything she thinks about and does, and which finds expression directly in the domestic scene. She can peel potatoes or plant a garden or scrub the kitchen floor with love, and with the same love. Her husband goes out into the great world and comes home again triumphant or beaten, or he just comes home, perhaps to be comforted and restored in the "act of love." But his wife has been in it all the time.

Whether these worlds can be shared or whether they slowly grow apart will depend to some extent on the natural awareness and sensitivity of the marriage partners. It depends also on whether, early in their married life, they established lines of communication. We have inherited a stereotype of the busy man who goes forth from his domestic castle into the world of affairs and comes home tired from the day's accomplishments, but unable to tell the "little woman" about them because she would not understand. Presumably she, too, has been busy, but on the whole with necessary though not very important things. Fortunately more and more people are finding this picture not only untrue but funny. The two worlds can be shared because women are people, not "little women." There are many interesting differences between men and women, but there is no difference between male and female intelligence. The late D. H. Lawrence says, in one of his *Assorted Articles*, "Man is willing to accept woman as an equal, as a man in skirts, as an angel, a devil, a baby-face, a machine, as instrument, a bosom, a womb, a pair of legs, a servant, an encyclopedia, an ideal or an obscenity; the one thing he won't accept her as is a human being, a real human being of the feminine sex."

Women have the same basic needs as men, and happy is the man who can say, "My wife is my friend." This man and this woman may not meet for long at breakfast, probably not at all for lunch, and supper may be punctuated by children's noises. But they do meet in bed and it is the best place to talk, to share the day's happenings, to become one again.

Love and Beauty

It is useless to say of a woman in love, "Whatever does she see in that man?" She sees the man she is in love with, and that is enough. We sometimes fool ourselves with our ideas of what is beautiful. The local, national, and world-wide beauty contests trap us, as well as the contestants and the anxious mothers, into believing that beauty can be so judged, or that static beauty (which is a gift of nature) is a thing good in itself when it meets some standard of measurement. Measuring beauty with a tape measure is about as sensible as measuring strength by a hammer-throw. Strength for what? For playing the violin? For heart surgery? For thinking clearly at a peace conference? For the daily attrition of living? The hammer-throw is an interesting thing to be good at, for an individual and for the people who watch it. But such an ability would not necessarily help its possessor to be a better husband or father of children or a grown-up human being. Nor would the ability to perform successful heart surgery. So with beauty. Beauty for what? With us it tends to be a success symbol as an end in itself—and frequently a heartbreak. Does it mean that the beauty, Miss Something-or-other, will be interesting to talk to at age forty? Or a warm and generous lover at thirty? Or a good companion at fifty? Or a well-proportioned bore at twenty-five?

Beauty is a quality, not a measurement. A loved person is beautiful because he or she is loved. Few would argue about physical attraction having a lot to do with the selection of a mate, but it is the beginning not the nourishing of the life together. And physical attraction can mean different things to different people. It is doubtless true that beauty is in the eye of the beholder; one is conditioned by the culture in which he lives, but he makes his own choice. It is not true that beauty is skin deep, unless what is meant is that beauty is an inner winsomeness which shines through various sizes and shapes of people, and not merely appearance. And while appearance changes, beauty lasts. It ripens with the years. John Donne's line is apt: "Nor spring, nor summer's beauty hath such grace as I have seen in one autumnal face."

Young people sometimes worry about the physical expression of married love when one is no longer young. They need not. Like other aspects of life together in the marriage bond this is a growing and deepening experience, and unless there is something wrong physically or psychologically it lasts a lifetime. One changes, of course, from the early days of imperious demand but a better thing takes its place, a deeper, more knowing union. It is true for many couples that the best years of their sexual lives come in middle age when the children have grown up and left home. There is a second honeymoon, a sort of Indian summer, of mature satisfaction and meaning.

No one is lovable all the time; and there are times when very well married people wish their husband or wife would just go away and stay there for a long time. We know, intellectually, that human beings love and hate each other at the same time, but we are usually pretty astonished when the hate is directed at good old innocent us! Christians have a resource here which the world in general does not have. We know that we are loved by a loving God when we are most unlovable; that is, when we need it most. And in that knowledge, that thanksgiving, we may be able to reach out, however gropingly, and find the person in whose body and spirit we can be whole again as God wants us to be whole.

7 · Children

SOMETIMES IT IS DIFFICULT TO REALIZE—LOOKING AROUND at the P.T.A. meeting, for instance—that parents of children were lovers before they were parents. But such is the case. These earnest, conservatively dressed, well-organized matrons and mates now serving on committees once said ridiculous things to each other in the moonlight. They listened to music and took romantic walks and dreamed the dreams of youth. They had plans and ambitions and rebellions. And they had one another—this special, golden, uniquely different person. Nothing would happen to their marriage as it had to so many others—the stodginess, the separate lives, the predictable monotony gently spiced with good causes, like raisins in the boarding house cake. And yet here they are sitting on folding chairs at the P.T.A. meeting. How did this come about? How were they trapped into this mazy place, this soft prison from which there seems no escape? The answer is easy: children! That is how it happened. One moment they were two young people speaking their love to each other as in the morning of the world; the next moment they are caught in a complex of diapers, baby-sitters, inconvenient housekeeping, and the 8:15. The early romantic days are over and the hopeful youngsters seem to have settled for business as usual, the business of being married, having children, living separate lives and touching hands occasionally as in a large, "other-directed" dance pattern.

Is there any help for this? They did not plan it this way or feel it this way. They had in fact looked forward to having children, had talked about it, hoped for it. When the young wife knew she was pregnant she was glad; a little afraid but mostly glad. ("Why when I was told the news, I felt wings upon my shoes.") In a way she seemed fulfilled, as if her womanhood had been justified. Her young husband was of two minds, but mostly proud and pleased about it. The old saying that a man wants a woman and a woman wants a baby is probably more true than not. The man has some unspoken fears of losing his wife, not only as a sexual partner for a while but, in a more subtle way, to a rival. And so it often happens. Especially so since our culture seems to worship the child. We have come a long way and perhaps a strange way from the Victorian household in which children were to be seen but not heard. Now the household seems to revolve around the child from the day of his birth, or before, through the TV age, the dating age, the school years, until the child leaves home to begin one of his own. During this twenty years or so the child's father, if typical, has never seemed to be around very much. In the early days he got home, usually tired, in time to see the children briefly before their bedtime. Day to day decisions affecting the children's lives—school problems, friends, recreation and discipline—fall mostly to mother. Later on when the pattern is noticed and worried about, it is set and hard to change. There is a varying amount of consultation between parents on matters of policy about the children, but in general the children seem to be running the show. It is their needs, their plans, their purposes which are served.

And God Made a Helpmeet . . .

Perhaps we had better go back a bit. If, as we have thought, the basic reason for the coming together of this man and this woman was to complete each other, then such a completing ought to take place before the family circle is enlarged. But it involves more than the passage of time. There is a mystery here, the mystery of freedom. How free is one to give himself away in such a demanding intimacy as marriage? How free is he or she to accept the gift of the other? The gift of the other's child? No other human relationship demands of the participants as much freedom as does a marriage. But there is a necessary order, a sequence of events, even though they overlap and minister to one another. First there is the love itself, the security of acceptance, the firm center. Then comes the enlargement of the loving group, the children. Finally and through all of this, there is the establishment of a home, a meeting place of hands and hearts and wills, an enduring thing, an island in time.

Here are some interesting words from the last (1958) meeting of the Lambeth Conference of Anglican bishops. For the rest of this section I shall follow the reasoning and use some of the words of the Lambeth report.

"The biblical revelation, however, does not limit the function of sexuality and the family to the reproductive purpose. Equally deep-rooted in *Genesis* is the reflection of a second factor—the need of man and woman for each other, to complement and fulfill each other and to establish a durable partnership against the loneliness and rigour of life. It was not good for man to be alone, and God made a helpmeet for him. The relationship of man and woman—of husband and wife—is rooted in God's creative purpose equally with the procreative function of sexuality. 'For this reason shall a man leave his father and mother and be joined to his wife.'

Thus in the heart of the biblical teaching about creation, two great insights into the nature and purpose of sexuality and the family are lodged. They are not subordinated one to the other; they are not directly related to one another; their relationship, in the developing experience of Israel, is to be found in yet a third area—that of the place of the family in giving responsible security to the children born of the love of husband and wife."

Family Planning

It follows, from the purpose of the family so described, that children might well be planned for as welcome guests in the circle of love and care. It is good to have children when one is young because it is easier physically and because one then has the enjoyment of their companionship. Responsible persons will guard against postponing having children until they have reached a certain financial goal or acquired a certain number of material things. They will also guard against bringing children into the world carelessly and improvidently, expecting unknown persons to provide for them, with little or no concern for the children or the society of which they are a part. Since one of the valid ends of marriage is the establishment of a union in love and trust between a man and a woman, it is not true to say that unless children are specifically desired, sexual intercourse is of the nature of sin. It is also wrong to say that such intercourse should not be engaged in except with the willing intention to procreate children. Another passage from the Lambeth report:

"It must be emphasized once again that family planning ought to be the result of thoughtful and prayerful Christian decision. Where it is, Christian husbands and wives need feel no hesitation in offering their decision humbly to God and following it with a clear conscience. The *means* of family planning are in large measure matters of clinical and aesthetic choice, subject to the requirement that they be admissible to the Christian conscience. Scientific studies can rightly help, and do, in assessing the effects and the usefulness of any particular means; and Christians have every right to use the gifts of science for proper ends."

When a Woman Has a Baby . . .

So when the hope for the gift of children issues forth into the creation of a new life, this child will be wanted, welcomed, provided for, and loved. Consider the miracle of birth. The planted seed finds lodging and grows silently until the appointed time. Slowly the woman's body becomes heavy with the fruit of her love. Quietly, as the day draws nearer, she is filled with a secret peace for she is being herself, and with an eagerness that her time may come soon for she is uncomfortable and expectant. Then the time does come, and in loneliness and anguish and deep joy a child is born. Jesus said, "A woman when she is in travail hath sorrow, because her hour is come: but as soon as she is delivered of the child, she remembereth no more the anguish, for joy that a man is born into the world. (*John 16:21*)

When a woman has a baby, it is just as much a miracle as the first day of creation. There *is* something new under the sun; a new life, a new being with all of its possibilities for good and evil, has come into the world. When the father and the mother of the child face each other after the event, they do so with mixed emotions: relief, thanksgiving, pride, hope, and a secret sobering feeling of a new responsibility. Here are some lines of verse by a modern mother.

> Come to term the started child shocks
> Peace upon me; I am great with peace;
> Pain teaches primal cause; my bones unlock
> To learn my final end. The formal increase
> Of passionate patience breaks into a storm of heat
> Where calling on you love my heart's hopes rise
> With violence to seize as prayer this sweet
> Submitting act. I pray. Loud with surprise
> Thrown sprung back wide the blithe body lies
> Exultant and wise. The born child cries.*

And a prayer, written by a young woman after the birth of her child and sent me by her husband.

O God, give us wisdom and grace to bring up this thy child and ours rightly and well, in love and trust and freedom, as thou hast taught us in Jesus Christ our Lord.

The birth of a child is the birth of hope. It is the parents' second chance, a projection into the future of their half-achieved purposes and meanings. At the same time it is a

* From *True Minds* by Marie Ponsot. (San Francisco: The City Lights Pocket Bookshop, 1956). Used by permission.

fostering, a nurture in all the best that one knows. There is nothing like the experience of watching a child develop from a little bundle of sensations to a candid, clear-eyed asker of questions. One realizes, somewhat frighteningly, that this is probably the closest he will ever come to being a custodian of the truth. A child has the priceless gift of wonder which so many adults lose, to their poverty. The world is new and interesting and strange, a place to be felt and explored, sometimes to be understood. To the open eyes of childhood it is a voyage of discovery, partly make-believe because that is a way one discovers himself, partly fact because that is a way one discovers necessary limits. It is never so open again, except to saints and poets. Someone has said that an adult is an obsolete child. To parents who have not forgotten how to wonder and to feel, the life of childhood can be shared to the enrichment of both.

God Has Not Grown Tired of Us

A Christian household shares with the world around it the same pulls toward disunity, the same selfishness, the same temptation to separatedness. But it has a self-knowledge which the world does not have, and special resources as well as special responsibilities. The Christian family knows that its fatherhood is in God, that its members can afford to be forgiving because they know themselves to be forgiven, that their love for one another is founded surely on God's steady love for them, which is stronger than an act of will, safer than the feeling of a moment. The responsibilities are reflections of the gifts. Here children will learn about God's love through the love of their parents for each other and for them. Better than by precept this will be breathed in with the air in that place, known through daily decisions and crises and courtesies. Children are great noticers and concluders, and one of the most effective educational devices in the world is the conversation which children overhear in their own homes. They will learn the privilege of shared pain and grief as well as shared joy. They will learn about judgment—where the pushed-out wall of one's life comes to a place that says No. They will learn, little by little, that other people have rights and privileges and freedoms to be cherished and defended as one's own. They will learn how to tell what things are important, how to distinguish the true and the right and the first-rate against the imitation and shoddy. They will learn how to speak fairly and to listen with courteous love. They will learn how to be themselves, in true individuality, and how to accept others in their equally true individuality, with patience and kindness. Deeds in a Christian family are done for love, not for gratitude which can be a form of slavery. So parents may grow up to be their children's friends.

There is no such thing as an ideal family any more than there is an ideal marriage. Normal troubles happen, normal strains and tensions often make us appear at less than our best. Business worries and personal disappointments shorten our tempers and distemper our courtesy. Physical weariness is the almost constant state of any mother of small children. We do not always hear what our children are saying, occasionally we do not even care. Sometimes we retreat behind the wall of our own selfishness posting a "Do Not Disturb" sign for any who would intrude. And it does happen that our children on whom we have lavished time and patience and loving care sometimes behave like something out of a jungle! But two facts remain for the Christian family:

first, that both they and we know better and can make another new start; secondly, that the resources which make our feeble love possible are still there. God, amazingly enough, has not grown tired of us and gone away.

It happens sometimes that couples who want very much to have children are physically unable to do so. This is a grief and a disappointment which can sometimes be helped by medical care. If not, a loving family can come into being through adoption. And many couples have found to their great joy that after having adopted a child they can have children of their own. Certainly for a man and wife who are childless it is a privilege to take the child of one who cannot keep it, and for the child to be so chosen may be his greatest blessing. Hopefully, a home should have children. They are often a burden, sometimes a trial, always unknown quantities—"hostages to fortune." But they are life; frequently sources of deep satisfaction, and good companions. There are certain stages through which one wonders if they will ever pass, and oneself survive. But they do, and so do we.

Parents always hope for the best in their children—that they will be healthy and normal, bright and beautiful. Sometimes this happens, and when it does such a family is a pleasure not only within itself but to everyone who knows them. But it does not always work out that way. Almost every family has some secret grief, a hurt, which they bear as well as they can and compensate for as well as they can. Often our problems need help from others. It is difficult for parents, especially young ones, to accept the fact that a seriously damaged child might be better off in the care of an institution than at home. Expert advice is necessary in these cases; and one cannot always be sure that he has done the right thing. Christian people say their prayers, listen to good counsel, and do the best they can. It is the same with personality and behavior problems. Make-believe on the parents' part will not help, nor will overprotection or sentimentalism. The key is love, not the romantic kind which is "blind," but the godly kind which sees and cares. In many cases there is nothing to be done in the sense of changing the situation, nothing except to live with it and learn through it and be as compassionate as one can be. We do learn things through these difficult experiences; it is one of the true ways of learning. We are not quite so ready with "answers" and we are a little more understanding of the problems of others. We can listen better and hear more.

When the hard problems come—the death of a child at birth or by accident, or the long hard pull of the situation that just has to be lived with day after day—then the Christian will fall back on the best he knows, the only answer to despair, which is that God makes himself known in the darkness as well as in the light, in anguish as well as in joy. The Lord, bearer of the world's pain and author of the world's joy, knows our hurts, our needs, our helplessness. He is our meeting place. Here is our comfort and our strength, the dwindling of our pride and, perhaps, the beginning of wisdom.

It Is Not Long . . . It Is Good

Happy is the child who has good memories of his childhood. They will last him all his life and when he is old he will think about them more and more. Family living has lots of problems, lots of ups and downs; but when it is open and loving it is one of the best things we can ever know. Years later when a family gathers for a wedding or a funeral or a family festival, the best part of the meeting will be the memories of good times and trying times, of shared tears and shared laughter. The kitchen is a good place for family reminiscences, especially if it has an old-fashioned kitchen table. It is near the source of supplies and, in a way, symbolizes the life of the family together. A family I know used to have a sort of board meeting every once in a while, in lean financial times, when there was a bit of extra money to be spent, sometimes as little as five dollars. They would meet around the kitchen table after a Sunday night supper of left-overs and discuss the problem, each one having a voice in the deliberations. On one of these occasions they decided to pool the resources and buy one of the daughters a new dress for her first real date. Of such things are family memories made.

It is not uncommon for us to spend so much time preparing for the future that we lose the present. Many fathers of families are hard at work day and night—sometimes on weekends too—providing good things, they would say, for the future, but who in the process lose the opportunity to know their own children. Some men tend to do this because business and office relationships are less intimate and therefore less demanding than family ones. But when it is too late it is too late; time flows only one way. In societies more primitive than our own, and perhaps closer to the earth, it was the father of the family who taught his son the skills of weapons and hunting on which his very life would depend. He was not only an authority figure, he was an authority and a necessary one. This is no longer true with us, but the symbol is just as valid. There are the skills of sports and of the basement workshop. There are daughters to be known as well as sons. Almost anyone can walk and explore, or fly a kite, or discover the fascinating life of a piece of the backyard turf, or the riches of the edge of the sea at low tide. Birds and trees and flowers and rocks have their own names and ways. Cities are honeycombs of interesting things to see and think about. Picnics and camping trips, even on a small scale, are revelations of nature and of ourselves. All that is really needed is a dash of imagination and a little time.

Children in a family are interestingly different and find their pleasures differently. Each one might be asked occasionally to plan an afternoon to be shared. Even the matter of discipline which so often falls to mother can, and ought to be, shared by father if he is there and involved. Children are seldom fooled. They know when the involvement is real, and out of these encounters companionship grows. The spectacle of a father saying to one of his children after years of being "busy," "Now let's you and I be real pals," is not an attractive one. It belongs in a cartoon. Companionship with children as with other people is a quiet thing and seldom happens head-on. One can discuss almost anything while winding up a kite string and watching the paper bird come slowly back to earth. One can talk about shy things easily while walking on a country road or in a city park, the footsteps making a companionable rhythm. The silences are easy because there is something else to do. One can do almost anything with companionship—except hurry it. There are times in a child's growing-up years when the thread seems to be lost, the openness closed, but if it was there in the early days it is still there and will come back in a different way when this corner has been turned.

It has been said that children begin by loving their parents, later on they judge them; but rarely, if ever, do they forgive them. This may be a bit strong yet it is certainly true that children see their parents the way they are. A college professor who was young enough to be ponderous engaged a student sitter for his two boys for an afternoon. When he and his wife came home they invited the college girl to stay for supper, which she did. During supper she made the mistake of asking her host a question relating to his academic field. He laid down his tools and obliged with a well illustrated reply which went on for some time. There followed a silence which one of the boys finally broke by remarking for the girl's illumination, "Daddy knows more, but Mommy knows better!"

The candor of children is occasionally terrifying but almost always refreshing. Recently I had Saturday night supper with a family I have known for several years. They knew I was coming back to town from a vacation spot for the weekend and had rescued me from my own cooking. It was an excellent meal and I remarked to the daughter of the house, aged twelve, that it was a much better meal than I would have had at home. She replied with delightful directness, "It's much better than we would have had, too."

One more. An elderly lady, who had grown comfortably plump, called during the summer on a younger couple whom she had not seen for some time. When the two children of the house appeared she felt called upon to make that strange remark, "My, how you have grown!" The children, quite understandably without an answer, retired to discuss the matter. They returned after a while to find their guest in conversation with their parents and addressed her solemnly, "Mrs. Smith, we think you have grown too!"

Time goes so fast in the growing up years. It seems no time at all since the children were babies. It is not long, the caring and the bearing and the joy. But it is good.

8 · Growing Up Together

A FEW YEARS AGO BEFORE TRAVEL WAS SO COMMON, TWO high-school boys planned a trip to New York City during their spring vacation. They had been planning it for some time and had thought about it constantly. The shining city was about five hours on the train from where they lived and this would be their first visit, in fact their first trip to any place so far away from their home town. Hours of delicious planning went into the preparations. Sober books from the library, a garish and well-thumbed folder from a bus company, travelers' tales from those who had actually been to Mecca, filled the imagination with beckoning possibilities. With just so much carefully hoarded money and just so much carefully budgeted time, would they spend it on the Empire State Building or on Radio City? How about Yankee Stadium as over against the Statue of Liberty? A carriage ride in Central Park (with a picture of it!) or balcony seats at a musical? And so it went. A few attractively envious classmates offered suggestions; others preserved an attitude of elaborate indifference. Nothing dampened the dream. Already the explorers anticipated reliving the golden hours at school lunch hour, aloud of course and casually. They had decided to go by bus and return by train; a dignified home-coming. Finally the eve of the great day arrived. The bags were packed and stood waiting by the door. . . . The telephone jangled in the middle of the night. It was the mother of one of the boys calling to say that her traveler had been rushed to the hospital for an emergency appendectomy. He was out of danger, greatly disappointed, but wanted his friend to take his share of the money and go for both of them. But it was no good. The glory had departed. What fun was a trip when there was no one to share it with?

Marriage is a shared trip through the years. Young married couples have already shared a number of trips before marriage, even if only to a bowling alley or a lunch counter or a school game. But each was or could be a voyage of discovery into the unknown land of another's personality. What observations could be shared? Did they think the same things were funny? What happened when everything did go wrong? How long did a sulk last? People who compile statistics about marriage tell us that the likelihood of a permanent union is increased when couples meet in a school or church situation, or both. It argues a community of interest about large important issues and attitudes, perhaps unspoken but none the less real. In an earlier chapter we thought of how we come to know one another gradually. So on these little excursions together we disclose ourselves by word and attitude, and on the basis of such experience we choose and are chosen.

The Romantic and the Practical

But there is another ground of meeting, not as individuals now but as men and women in general. We seem to have been victimized by a lie which we know to be a lie when we think about it, but which we continue to accept and act upon as if it were true. For some reason the legend has grown up among us that women are romanticists and that the men are the practical people of the world. Nothing could be farther from the truth. Many writers much wiser than I have speculated about the roots of this legend in our cultural past. The image already alluded to of the "little woman" whose pretty little head cannot be bothered with the facts of real life is amazingly persistent. And this in the face of the facts that she is increasingly a college graduate and probably *can* read a book, that she gets the meals, bears the children, acts as shock absorber and balance wheel in the cares and frets of the household.

The man's point of view, exaggerated a bit, might go something like this. A man busy with his workaday world but uninspired by it dreams a dream. Someday, he says to himself, I shall go to the South Seas, perhaps on a raft of balsa wood. Never having been to the South Seas he pictures himself wading ashore, tanned and healthy, to be greeted by friendly and beautiful natives bearing baskets of ripe fruit. Smiling secretly to himself he goes to a lumber yard on a Saturday, assembles mysterious supplies, and begins work in the basement. He is happy. One evening some time later he is smoking a pipe contentedly in the basement with one of his neighbors who also has dreamed of sailing to the South Seas. His wife appears at the top of the stairs. She looks solid and real. No palm trees sway in her mind's eye.

"What," she demands, "are you doing?"

"We're making a raft to go to the South Seas."

"You are not," she says. "I thought you might be fixing the water heater, but that's probably too much to expect."

The door closes. The dream fades. The neighbor says,

"Well, I guess I'd better be getting along. See you, Tom."

Now we might look at it the other way. Here is a housewife (she sometimes feels as if she were indeed the wife of the house!), intelligent and interested in many things but with little time to pursue them. She tries not to go to seed intellectually, to keep up with some of her old interests in the arts, or tennis, or gardening. Some of this may be fitted into odd moments, and frequently is, but women often feel that in the first ten years of the marriage they are at a disadvantage. They get left behind. There are these walls and these children and these many demands. One gets too tired to read anything much but stories with machine-made plots. Even so, women in general are more literate than men. And it is fun to go out once in a while and leave these walls—not a large adventure, just a small one. Dinner and dancing perhaps, or a show, or some interesting people to talk with about interesting things. Later it may turn out that it would have been more enjoyable to stay home, but at least one's opinion would then be based on some evidence. But so often when the man gets home from the day at the office, usually after a commuting trip, he would like to take his shoes off and stay there.

Both of these needs are real—sailing to the South Seas, and going out to dinner. Part of the difference is in the size of the dream. Most men are incurable romanticists. It is true, more often than not, that the dream lives and dies only in the imagination. The pathways of history are dotted with the ruins of Utopias, though as Oscar Wilde remarked, "A map of the world that does not include Utopia is not worth even glancing at." But some come home under full sail, with banners flying and trumpets sounding, to the enrichment of the whole human race. So Columbus, leaving the Pillars of

Hercules behind him, sails through real and imaginary terrors to an unknown land. So Einstein voyages out onto the planed surfaces of time and space. So the great plays and poems and symphonies are written, the great dreams of peace and brotherhood dreamed. So the atom is split, Everest climbed, the globe circled. And men *do* sail to the South Seas on a raft of balsa wood.

Some of the traditional differences between men and women are cultural and changing. There was a time not long gone when young women were discouraged from pursuing "higher" education because their delicate constitutions could not support the heavy burden of so much study! Many jobs and professions were closed to women because it was presupposed that they could not be successful at them. I think we can say two things here. The first is that when we have understood as well as we can the reasons for cultural and changing differences between men and women, their views of themselves and each other, there remains the fundamental and permanently characteristic difference between romanticist and realist. Some women do write plays and poems, and good ones. Women are among the great teachers and physicians and business executives. It is equally true that men are among the world's great cooks and dress designers. But perhaps it is not too much to say that a man so engaged is at least in part being a romanticist. More women are good cooks than great ones. Some women are able successfully to combine marriage with a professional career, but it does not seem to be the general rule. Characteristically, women do not sail to the South Seas, not because they would not survive as well or better than the men, but because it would not occur to them to do so. They are too sensible to try anything of the kind. And many women who have successful careers would prefer to be well married and are frank enough to say so.

My second observation is that in a creative marriage relationship the romantic and the practical complement and complete each other as in the physical union. They are not exclusive worlds; they support each other. Two things are necessary: that the lines of communication between the two (persons and worlds) be kept open: that there is a willingness for the two (persons and worlds) to understand and interpret each other, and there is mutual respect for the other (person and world) as unique and important. Strangely enough, one of the places where the romantic and practical roles are reversed is at dinner, where women prefer the flattering reflection of candlelight and men are expected to pretend that there is insufficient light for the familiar process of eating.

It is interesting to note that while our roles as men and women change somewhat with cultural changes, they are essentially those which we have always known. Primitive man hunted wild beasts to provide food and clothing for the family, while his woman kept the cave and took care of the children. Contemporary man goes out into the jungle of business or professional life and does battle for the family necessities, while his woman keeps house and takes care of the children. Man has always been the adventurer, the seeker of better hunting grounds, greener pastures, more fertile valleys. So now he is apt to be the restless partner, the wanderer, the speculator. A woman's instinct is to improve the cave, to put roots down in the neighborhood and the community. Women do not usually enjoy impersonal work as men often do; they want to work *for* someone—a husband, a child, a boss, the good of a specific neighborhood or community. Men can work for an idea, a principle, or to change the world. Women are more adaptable, better at improvising. Children in a family can remember many quick repairs made by mother, swiftly and with makeshift means, which served the purpose at the essential moment. Father would want more time and the proper tool, by which time the particular pressing need would probably have passed.

The Constant Adjusting of Two Egos

Men cherish routines, sometimes elaborate ones, and habitual ways of doing things. They tend to carry the same things in the same pockets. They are more easy to describe than women. They are more predictable. On the whole a man knows before he enters a store what it is he wants to buy; a woman discovers what she wants after she is inside. Men are more boastful, women more personal. In an argument two men can disagree strongly and remain good friends, while it is easy for a woman to take such a disagreement personally. The personal-impersonal difference carries over into groups of men and women. In a mixed group women often congregate to talk about clothes, children and cooking, immediately and in personal terms. At another place in the same room the men will likely be discussing either an object or an issue, but more impersonally. The women will probably be seated, the men standing in a loose sort of circle. When men sit down in a small group the talk gets more personal—"I remember the time that . . ." This general difference was formalized in the Victorian custom of the women withdrawing after dinner for conversation presumably appropriate to them (echo in the contemporary women's bridge party, perhaps?), while the men brightened up with port and cigars and bluff manly talk. At the ceremonial signal from the host—"Shall we join the ladies?"— they put down their cigars and, in an aura of shared masculinity, sauntered into the drawing room to see what the ladies had been bothering their pretty heads about.

There may have been a loss in the passing of the frank recognition of these separate worlds. Some serious observers think so, pointing out that modern man in the Western world has lost his manliness in a society which has become largely matriarchal. Women, they tell us, control most of the spending money since they are the taste-makers in an increasingly affluent society; they tend to live longer and so inherit the insurance money; they are the financial beneficiaries of a divorce; they organize everything, including husbands. But the fact is that few women really wish to dominate, and if a husband is henpecked it is largely his own fault. The important point for us here is that in a free and creative marriage the two worlds do not have to be divisive. Given the basic fact of the permanence of the temperamental differences, they *can* be the stuff of warfare and, in any marriage, will occasionally be the reason for skirmishes. But recognized and admitted, they can be the grounds of a shared experience. It is easy for us to fall into the trap of loose generalities about "all men" and "all women." One is not married to all men or all women but to this particular man or woman. The real question for them is, where do *their* two worlds meet?

What we are thinking about is the adventure and interchange of a man and a woman growing up together. Love does not happen all at once. It begins with attraction and continues with attention but it has to be lived out, which means time and patience and gentleness. Attraction comes like a flash, love takes longer. Love at first sight, a doubtful phenomenon, means attraction at first sight which proved later to be more than that. A marriage is the beginning of the possibility of married life and love together. Many couples think they are in love when actually they are not even acquainted. They know only the symbol, the image, of this other person in their own eyes. No conflict has arisen, no worlds clash; this other person is, in a sense, invented and the invention is represented by a name. The fact that marriage is a process of constantly adjusting two egos as well as exchanging two solitudes often does not occur to couples until after they have been joined together to follow a common path. This is just as true in a good sense. Given a small community of ideas, interests, and attitudes, and a little time, a married couple will wonder after a while how they could have thought they were in love a year ago. So much has happened, deepened, unfolded in the meantime to give the word meaning.

When a man says to a woman, "I love you," and means it, he cannot possibly make the words hold what he wants them to hold. The words are symbols of a meaning in the heart and mind and will. Here again is the sacramental nature of marriage, the things that stand for meanings—words, actions, shared experience. So the act of sexual union which joins together a man and a woman in one flesh can be a sacramental way of saying "I love you" better than any words. But the "I love you" is a text, a preface, a preamble for all aspects of these two lives growing up together. They will meet in many expected and unexpected ways; in the daily bread of tears and laughter, in praying together and worrying together, and eating pickles together on a mountain top.

Remembering and Self-disclosure

When two young people begin married life they usually seem to the next older generation, their parents for instance, very young indeed. But they probably do not feel young to themselves, so much has happened. They may feel quite wise. And already in their coming to know each other they have tried to share some of their separate experience, to disclose scenes of various persons and events which in some way seem important. People in love enjoy hearing about one another's remembered moments.

Why do we remember the things we do remember? What makes them linger in our memories, and when they well up in our conscious mind how can we let another person see them as we see them? I think that a person's memory is the core of himself, his identity to himself. He will be recognized by his friends when he walks into a room because he looks like that. He will be remembered by his friends as he looked, probably at a certain time, but more clearly as he *was*, in terms of a word or a happening or a reaction. So a man remembers himself and, in telling about it, defines himself. A man says to his wife at some moment of reflective quiet together, "You know, that reminds me of something that happened to me when I was a kid visiting on a farm. I never forgot it." Or the young wife on a similar occasion, "I didn't have much confidence in myself, and my sister Pat had so much. I was never very good at games; I guess that's why I read all the books in the house. Some of them I used to puzzle over for weeks." So the subtle process of self-disclosure goes on and two people share themselves with one another in the eye of memory. All human beings invent things which did not really happen, at least not in just that way. Little boys invent "My Uncle" stories that make Superman look like a failure. Many people invent romantic episodes out of loneliness or successful ones out of insecurity.

But I am not thinking of that sort of thing now; I am thinking, rather, of the incident or impression that really happened and which stays with a person all his life. If you were to put this book down right now and let your mind drift slowly like a leaf on a stream, you would doubtless be reminded of some little incident which you have treasured for years. When families do this together, as on some of the occasions we thought about in the last chapter, there sometimes come fresh disclosures after many years. "I never knew you thought that," or "I never knew you knew." The newly married couple remembering together is one of the best ways of growing together, of becoming one.

Significant events in one's personal history remembered for a lifetime are often difficult to explain because, put into words, they do not seem very eventful. The high moment, the rare penetration into things as they are, may last but a second and may take place in the most commonplace circumstances: the look on a child's face "holding wonder like a cup," the casual word of a friend who was not even trying to be wise, the ring of young laughter on a boat trip when things were so beautifully right for a moment one could almost weep for the joy of it, a strain of music heard for the first time which opened a golden door into a delightful land. Sometimes the important events are silent, speaking only in the inner dialogue of the spirit. One recalls Ezra Pound's haunting lines:

> Nathless I have been a tree amid the wood,
> And many a new thing understood
> That was rank folly to my head before.

There are some things seen by memory's eye which cannot be shared because one does not have the words for them or perhaps does not understand their meaning. There may be some shy places one is not yet ready to revisit. But the growing together and the growing up together can be shared in this way as in no other.

That's How You Know It's George

Stephen Benét once wrote a wise and delightful tale of married life called *The Story About the Ant-eater*. It has to do with an anecdote told by the young man to his fiancée on a sultry, tension-filled afternoon shortly before the day of the wedding. She was not amused. In fact hot words were exchanged and tempers stretched almost to the breaking point before the return of some measure of sanity and good humor saved the day. But she never did like that story and there were times in the years ahead when she thought that if she heard Roger tell it once more she would die. But he did, of course, and she did not. Several years later she asked an older woman who had been married much longer if she had had the experience of hearing the same story so many times she could hardly stand it. Benét goes on:

"A gleam of mirth appeared in Mrs. Lattimore's eyes.

'My dear,' she said, 'has George ever told you about his trip to Peru?'

'No.'

'Well, don't let him.' She reflected. 'Or, no—do let him,' she said. 'Poor George—he does get such fun out of it. And you would be a new audience. But it happened fifteen years ago, my dear, and I think I could repeat every word after him verbatim, once he's started. Even so—I often feel as if he'd never stop.'

She put her hand on the younger woman's arm.

'We're all of us alike, my dear,' she said. 'When I'm an old lady in a wheel chair, George will still be telling me about Peru. But then, if he didn't, I wouldn't know it was George.'"

Does this sound like your house? Most husbands and many wives have ant-eater stories which the other could repeat word for word, with exactly the same dramatic pauses and the identical punch line. But after a few years of living together—that's how you know it's George. Some of the sharp edges of our criticalness wear off and we begin to become a little easier to live with. Grown-up-ness does not come in a night, nor patience in a morning; but they do come. It is sometimes rather a long road from dancing till dawn to bearing one another's burdens, but it can be found and traveled together. Love begins at a meeting, it is pledged on the day of the wedding, it grows in the living of it.

9 · Relatives, Friends, and Rivals

No man is an island, nor is any marriage, though it is customary and rather attractive for a newly married couple to feel like a closed corporation against the world. They have found each other and for a while this is enough. There is much to explore and discuss and decide. There is a house or an apartment to be settled, provided for and enjoyed. Some of the wedding presents are displayed proudly, some put away for future use, some sequestered in a closet till one can think what to do with them. But the place is now "ours." Slowly it begins to take on the color of our personalities, to feel like home, to be the place where remembered events took place. One of the charms of an old house where generations of the same family have lived out their days is this effect of a stage-set with many rooms and many scenes: angry words and loving ones, weddings and funerals, parties, reunions and solitary midnight meditations, tragedies and comedies. The history of a family in a house, whether large or small, begins at some point with the arrival of a man and his wife wondering what life in this place is going to be like.

The difference between a new living place and an old one is the difference of personal investment. A new place is simply a new place, untried, unexperienced. Years later, or even months, it has taken on the familiarity of an old friend, including the things that don't work. It has been lived in, used, criticized and enjoyed. It has been the setting for early joys and early misunderstandings, early gropings toward a living pattern. No couple ever forget their first place. It may have been inconvenient, probably was. It may have been scantily furnished, or poorly heated, too small or too large, but it was the place where the new life together began. Gradually the circles of living go out from this center. New paths are made to old friends, new neighbors who may become friends are met and speculated about. The street becomes *our* street with known trees and familiar house fronts, some of which remain only that while others become gateways to friendships that will last a lifetime.

Relatives

One of the adventures of married life is that of getting to know the family of one's husband or wife. They are usually a mixed bag; some of them one accepts, and is accepted by immediately, while others take some getting used to. One tends to view his own family and friends through the eyes of love, or at least through the eyes of familiarity. If Uncle Bill or Brother Tom or Aunt Jane are a bit strange or difficult to understand they have been that way for a long time and one makes peace with it, like the weather. Some interpretation may be necessary to one's marriage partner. On the other hand, it may happen that a relative originally viewed with some alarm will turn out years later to be a firm friend and a wise companion. It is not unusual for people old enough to be married to feel as close to brothers- and sisters-in-law as to their own brothers and sisters. In the process of growing up in a family brothers and sisters do not automatically love one another! In fact there are times when they consider one another strictly expendable; and harried mothers, once more separating the combatants, feel the same. It takes a few years, sometimes a separation, for brothers and sisters to appreciate each other. By the time they arrive at marrying age both they and their new in-laws are old enough to have become relatively civilized and meet on that basis without the strife of growing up together.

A person spends most of his growing-up years trying to discover who he is and what he wants. Precept and example, trial and error of experience, deliberate imitation of others, all go into this process, as well as the long quiet sessions of speculation and wondering. Most people can remember their own strainings against authority in their teens, in most cases a necessary rebellion, as growing pains in the process of self-knowledge. We try to close the gap between what we feel to be ourselves and what others seem to feel about us. A child seems to be one person to his father but another to his mother, and so on with his relation to schoolteachers, younger and older brothers and sisters, grandparents, a best friend, an "enemy." He sometimes wonders who *he* is in the midst of all these relationships. Along the way he discovers ways of self-expression with which to define himself, likes and dislikes, resources of various kinds. To one person athletic equipment will seem familiar the first time he picks it up, while to another it will always remain baffling. One will find himself at home with books; another will view them as necessary evils. Most people learn some of the laws of criticism and a smaller number learn how to criticize themselves helpfully. By the time we come to marry, each of us has become to a large extent the person he will continue to be.

This is the person who falls in love, discovers a congenial companion and forms a little community of shared interests and attitudes. This is the beginning, the initial commitment of the marriage contract. The married couple's life together and their shared life with others goes out from here.

Friends

Those who have been married for a number of years can look back on a gallery of neighbors and acquaintances, friends and fiddlers, in this place and that along the way. A few good friends last through the whole journey, especially if the friendship is kept in repair by occasional meetings. One leaves an old familiar place with regrets partly for the place itself but even more for some of the people there. Then after a while the new place becomes familiar and the couple find themselves with a new circle of friends and acquaintances. The marriage itself begins with a friendship and the wider circle is an extension of the original one. Interests shared between husband and wife are offered to a wider group. People share the enjoyment of singing together in choirs and other groups, the companionship of bowling and tennis and card playing. Some meet because of a mutual interest in some art or craft or to pursue interesting hobbies. There are married people who can escape television viewing long enough to discover the pleasure of reading aloud. It sometimes happens that one will have a real gift this way, greatly to the delight of family and friends. Some books ask to be read aloud. There are neighborhood groups of congenial people who enjoy reading plays together, with different members taking parts. And there are still those who gather to make their own music.

There is no reason why a husband or wife should not have friends unknown to the other or known less well. Interests vary among people and with the same people at different times. As long as the marriage community is firm at the center and conversation easy, new views and insights and experiences can be brought home to be shared. It sometimes happens that outside activities and people become more interesting than those at home. This may be because one of the partners has grown more than the other since the marriage began. Or it may be the result of boredom. The marriage is no longer new and exciting. Explorations of the early days have been replaced by known ways, familiar patterns, and more settled times. The old phrase "to get married and settle down" can be understood in two ways. It may mean that one's questing days are happily over and a mate has been found with whom one wishes to walk the ways of the world, the person with whom one wishes to share his bread and his body, his dreams and his defeats. Or the settling down may be of a different kind, a sort of resignation in the face of the fact that romance is over, that everything including sex is a routine and the marriage a convenient but colorless living arrangement. Actually, no two marriages are as different as these two descriptions. Much of anyone's life is humdrum and routine, and of anyone's marriage. Some index to one's emotional maturity is to be found in the manner in which he endures monotony. It is a common experience for married couples to discover that they have slipped, without noticing it, into little grooves of habit and predictability. They even come to say the same things habitually, the same old phrase which once had some point but is now threadbare with too much use. Here the friends may help, perhaps new ones. It may be that this husband and wife need a general stock taking to see where they are. It may have been years since they have done so, and now a bit difficult to start. But the possible alternative now is that the marriage, uncriticized and unobserved in the other's presence, will slowly fade away. It would be a mistake to be *too* observant. One can do himself a disservice by constantly taking his emotional pulse, and the same is true of a marriage. On the other hand there is nothing automatic or guaranteed about a good marriage. It needs to be cared for as any other human relationship needs to be cared for. Perhaps a new recreation can be found with one or two other congenial couples, or a neighborhood project, or a short trip. An overnight in a different place will sometimes break the chain of days.

One of the ways married couples come to meet one another is through their children. This begins even before nursery school days, perhaps by way of a car pool; but it really gets into stride when the children are old enough to bring their friends home after school in the endless quest for something to eat and for the fascination of seeing the inner workings of another person's house. Most of us remember with gratitude the houses in which we knew we were welcome as children. Those wonderful neighborhood mothers who accepted us the way we were without too much effort to improve us, who did have a cookie jar and who talked to us as if we were people. And of course it is always more fun to dry the dishes in a kitchen other than one's own. Many groups of parents in neighborhood, church, or school meet accidentally or regularly because of the involvement of their children in various activities. Some of these turn out to be lasting friendships, living long after the reason for their beginning, and independent of it.

Some of the hospitable people whom we remember lovingly all our lives were not married. Their open-door policy may have been a conscious or unconscious substitute for not having families of their own; but in the cases I remember best I would say that they were just interesting people with a gift for friendship. All of the interesting people do not get married. Some who would be delightful marriage companions and wonderful parents of children for one reason or another stay single. They should be gathered in by families to the benefit of all. Many of us have known the warmhearted unmarried woman with the friendly kitchen, and some courtesy aunts and uncles. There is an opportunity here in the opposite direction. Families happy in their own security may reach out and claim an unmarried man or woman as a loved and honored guest who is thus both blessed and blessing. I think of the rare person, claimed happily by two or three families, whose visits are keenly anticipated and warmly remembered; the rare soul who not only remembers the children's birthdays but remembers with exactly the right thing; the person of loving perception in whose good company the children open like flowers and feel tall, who brings a dimension of living to the household which warms and spices it.

Everyone knows something about loneliness, the curse of mankind, the problem of the unrelated self. Each of us can remember some particular instances of loneliness when we felt more than usually isolated. There is the fearful emptiness a child feels when he knows he is lost. It is bad in a quiet place like a woods or an unfamiliar countryside, perhaps even worse in a public place full of unknown people. After many years I can vividly recall losing track of my grandfather who had taken me to the zoo. There seemed to be hundreds of people, mostly children and their parents, looking into cages and talking excitedly, eating popcorn out of paper bags. What I remember chiefly is their backs; a frightened little boy searching frantically between rows of backs, stopping every few feet to ask in a shaky voice, "Have you seen my grandfather?" People in the warmest of families, both children and adults, know loneliness at times, sometimes a deep sense of it. But for the single person, unless he or she is unusually well fortified, there are many times when the world seems to be made up mostly of unconcerned backs. It is not so much that they do not care, though this is often true, as it is that they are so occupied with their own concerns that they do not notice anything else. It is easy for us not to notice, but in so doing we cheat not only the person who might be invited in but ourselves as well. A person may know, theoretically, that he is beloved of the Lord; yet unless there is someone here and now to speak to him in the Lord's name, the knowledge is not very useful to him. Although a person may be highly competent in his field, even greatly admired, it is not always a good substitute for being invited to supper. I know a family who make a regular custom of a guest night, when a person is invited to the family table and made a member of the circle for the evening. It may be a newly met or a newly noticed person, or one forgotten until something brings him to mind. It sometimes turns out to be a failure but not often, and it ministers both ways. It is a welcome for a stranger and one of the best ways I know of meeting the problem of the family settling into its own same little grooves.

Rivals

This brings us to the problem of the special friend who may become too special. In an earlier chapter we thought of the question as raised by young people about the possibility of meeting The One after marriage. That was a speculation; what we are considering now is a fact. Let me overstate it a bit for the sake of both brevity and clarity. Suppose an ordinary couple, who meet in one of the ordinary ways, marry each other and settle into a community, survive the strains of the early years together, put down roots, have children, get bored with one another occasionally, remember sometimes their unencumbered days, are frequently tired, often irritated by the children. The man finds his job fairly interesting but not very exciting; he has fallen into a routine. He wishes he made more money and sometimes feels that he has been passed over for promotion when men of lesser ability and value to the company have been moved up. His wife does not always appear to understand why he seems unable to "do something about it," and she agrees that more money would be a help. He looks at his wife and wonders what has become of her charm. She is a good wife to him in a familiar sort of way, rather ordinary. He doesn't think of doing foolish things with her as they once did. He wonders why. She is undoubtedly a good mother, and the children take up most of her time. It looks like a long road ahead and a dull one at that. That's life, he thinks.

The wife looks up from her sewing and glances at her husband. He used to be a forceful, energetic person, she reflects, with visions of a bright future. Perhaps he is losing his grip. They have agreed without saying so not to talk about it; it never seems to get them anywhere. In the silence of her own mind she wonders why their marriage is not what it used to be. She is busy with the children most of the time, seems to spend a large part of her life planning and shopping for meals, getting them and cleaning up afterward.

When her husband feels romantic, it is a quick thing and she is usually too tired anyway. Love's bright dream does not last forever, yet somehow she did expect marriage to be better than this. It looks like a long road ahead with a gradual loss of good looks, perhaps the inevitability of a matronly figure and sensible shoes.

And so the stage is set for the attractive stranger. Let us look at the picture first from the husband's point of view, then from the wife's. The attractive stranger turned up at a party, invited because she was the friend of someone and had recently moved to town to take a job. My, she was a stunner! Good looking, well dressed, charming figure, bright and witty and interested in everything. Almost as if by prearrangement their eyes meet in a moment of silence and there seems to be a secret understanding, as if they had always known each other, as if they had been waiting to meet. For a few seconds they seem to be alone together in the room. They drift into conversation, finding common ground easily and smoothly. Everything goes well. Life picks up again. It has meaning, it has content, it has beauty. This woman knows who he really is. There is a possibility of a real meeting. If he thinks of his wife at all just now it is fleetingly; she is probably exchanging recipes with somebody.

In this brief encounter I am not thinking of straight seduction, which is the phenomenon of attention focused with skill and perhaps with experience as an end in itself. A gentleman has been described as a patient wolf and most men, at least in imagination, will remain predatory in this respect until they die. At any age men relinquish only with the greatest reluctance the belief that they are charming to women of any age. What we have here is a collection of quite ordinary elements combined in such a way as to increase the possibility of explosion: vanity, boredom, need for self-assurance, imagination of man the romanticist, and challenge. Writing on this subject in an essay on Robert Burns, himself a man of some experience in these matters, Robert Louis Stevenson says that he thinks the spark is challenge. It is as if this attractive woman with the dark snapping eyes were saying, "Do you dare venture out from your snug domesticity to dance with me in the moonlight?"

Now let us think about the wife. On some occasion which promised in advance to be just like many similar occasions she meets a man who makes her feel like a woman, an attractive and desirable one. It is a good feeling and she enjoys it. She may have been placed next to him at a supper party, or the meeting might take place quite accidentally in the course of volunteer work at the hospital or the local church. In any case there has been a recognition. A light has been struck illuminating, in a tiny flash, a host of possibilities. None of them is named yet, not even in the mind; but as the attractive stranger talks interestingly and smiles pleasantly, there is a stirring of old powers in her. She has kept her looks and her figure and now she is glad. Her eyes brighten. She begins to respond. For a moment they seem to be alone together wherever they are. This man knows who she really is. There is a possibility of a real meeting. She would like to go for a long walk with him and talk about a hundred things. If she thinks of her husband at all just now it is fleetingly; he is probably talking to somebody about sump pumps.

We might call this the phenomenon of rediscovery. One thinks sometimes of old loves, of the persons one might have married and did not. A woman speculates on what might have happened if she had married Jack instead of Bill.

When she first met Bill (it seems such a long time ago) he was the one who seemed to know who she was, how she felt, what she meant when nobody else did. That was really how they came to fall in love, and it was that understanding which was expressed in their married love. They met. What seems to have happened now is that there is less to meet about, less to express, too much routine, too many things to do, so little time. And now comes this fascinating man who makes her feel young and alive again. Is such a chance to be missed? How is it to be handled? Not being a hopeless romanticist, she knows good and well that she and the attractive stranger are not going to join hands and dash off with no luggage to the Spice Islands or to a castle in Spain. But she is grateful. He seems to be saying, "Will you put away your sewing and your everlasting practicality for a golden moment? Will you risk your domestic tranquility to be for a moment the intensely alive and lovable person I know you to be?" The heart belongs to him who knows it best.

What shall we say about this? It would be silly to pretend that it does not happen, and to the "best people." It would be silly to pretend that it is not sometimes quite genuine. Some of the "great loves" of history began in just such a way. No one is safe against this sort of attack because he has a certain name or position or because he thinks the proper thoughts. We are all vulnerable because we are human beings with bodies, parts and passions, with needs and desires. Is it merely chance? I am sure that we cannot lay down a set of rules to be followed successfully in all cases; we can, perhaps, raise some questions and make some observations about what is really here. In the first place the encounter is not bad in itself. It is the sort of thing that happens without invitation, at least on the conscious level. And it is real. Like any other temptation it is a fork in the road where one has to choose his way and can do so. It is true that people may become so passionately involved in one another that nothing else matters at all, but not now, not at the moment of meeting. There is still time, one is still standing at the fork in the path. Further, it is only honest to say that we are dealing in this encounter with an idealized picture. This man we meet at dinner who has such a charming voice and such elegant manners, the delightful stranger whom we meet some other way, who makes one feel so vibrantly alive and important—we do not have to look at him in his pajama bottoms at seven o'clock in the morning, or pick up his clothes, or hear his ant-eater story for the ninety-seventh time, or listen to him snore. And so with the woman of dark beauty and infinite charm who invited us to dance with her in the moonlight. How would she look in a faded house dress with three crying children and someone at the door? How would she look in hair-curlers at seven o'clock in the morning? We seem to have gone back to the romantic dream of young love before the Fall. And so we have. It should not surprise us, but it does. And it is not easy to think of these things at the moment, especially when one does not wish to do so.

The trouble with either being or having a mistress is that the better it is the worse it is. The love may be quite genuine. Who can say? But it can never be said out loud. It must live in a twilight zone of secrecy and deception, and eventually it comes to feed upon itself because it has nothing else to feed upon. The woman in the case has no status which is definable in our culture. She is not usually a wife, though she may become one at the expense of a broken home. She is not a prostitute, nor a concubine. She is nothing and nobody but a woman in love with a man she cannot claim. She may be better off for having known love—she would probably say so—but it costs a lot and there is no surety about it. The man may move away or find someone else or change his mind or be discovered. Having said all that, if a woman is in love she is in love and all the arguments in the world will not make the slightest difference. But she might listen to her other self before she takes the trip.

Human relationships are subtle and changing but they move in certain patterns. For instance, the relationship between a father and his son changes in many ways over the years, but through all the changes one is still father and the other still son. So again, in an office situation one has a set of relationships in which he is free to move, or in a neighborhood. One has a role which gives him the ability to relate to people in other roles as long as the roles are accepted. But when the pattern is broken, by having an "office wife" for instance, the old free relationship is gone, yet the new one cannot be acknowledged or enjoyed. They must be strangers when they meet.

Married people sometimes report returning from brief encounters refreshed and renewed, better able to cope with difficult situations. This may be true; many things can be understood after an event which would not have been recommended before it. Even so, quite apart from moral and religious considerations, it is a risky emotional way to deal with an existing marriage relationship, and a dangerous way in which to begin a new one. Let us go back to the family group welcoming strangers into its circle of love and concern. This is good both ways, and it is the secure family who will feel free to do so. When there is genuine love, then there is genuine love and it is of God. But there are many ways of expressing it. People who love each other can express it in many ways other than going to bed together. This is a good way, perhaps the best, but it says too much to be casual about it when it is outside the bounds of social and religious sanction. Inside it can never say too much; outside it says more than can be supported, since it is impossible to live it out. People who feel strongly drawn to the attractive stranger—and it can be very strong—are sometimes helped by talking it over with a trusted third party, perhaps a clergyman or a marriage counselor. Sometimes in intelligent self-defense people have to agree not to meet in circumstances which might be dangerous. The old rolling (and precise) phrase in moral theology speaks of avoiding the occasion of proximate sin. Sometimes it is a help for them to talk it over frankly between themselves instead of just letting things happen, admitting their desire as well as the inadvisability of expressing it physically. There are hundreds of good sexual relations between men and women, sex with a small "s" so to speak, which are not dangerous. In this good sense all relationships between men and women are sexual relationships. But they are not committing ones. Such relationships may last a lifetime—good friendships between married and unmarried men and women—and are a blessing and a benefit to all parties.

This brings us back to the young married couple founding a home and beginning their good life together. It will be a tapestry with many colors and many textures, a living place with many scenes and movements. Many people will contribute to it, hopefully many will be blessed by it. The best thing we ever know is family love and the friends who gather around its warmth.

10 · Trouble

TROUBLE SEEMS TO HAVE A RATHER GENERAL DISTRIBUTION.
The author of *The Book of Job* says that man is born for
trouble as the sparks fly upward, without specifying whether
man in this case is married or unmarried. One suspects that
it makes little difference. Trouble in marriage is very much
like trouble any other place but perhaps a bit more difficult to escape. A wife, husband, or child is frequently a tar-
get for frustration for no other reason than simple availabil-
ity. The arena is defined, and the same elements that can
be used for the building of a happy marriage can be used for
destructive purposes. I know of no marriage where this does
not happen in some degree. We forget sometimes that love
is a grace not a remedy, that marriage is a life together not
a problem-solver.

Recently, in San Francisco, a sidewalk interviewer with
a recording device asked a number of men and women what
was the biggest adjustment in marriage. I have a copy of the
replies of eight of them, all married, and while it is not a
large body of data the answers seem representative of what
Americans think about marriage adjustments. The first
thought was that the biggest adjustment was to the loss of
independence, the necessity of taking into account the feel-

ings of another person, especially in the area of finances. This was spoken by a man but it is true these days of women in that many girls have jobs before they marry and have enjoyed temporary independence, even though they are willing to exchange it. The second spoke of conflicting wants and tastes in one's partner, using spending money as an example. The third reporter said, "Before, if a man got the whim to go have a beer with the boys, he went. Now he has to think of the little woman (there she is again!) worrying if he doesn't show up when she says." He added that they had to get used to each other's idiosyncrasies, and that the engagement period is not a realistic trial because each is at his courteous best. Another (a man) recommending tolerance, especially in little habits that annoy, added, "The average man is bullheaded, so in most cases the wife ends up doing the compromising." The fifth reply, contrary to the third, said that the period of adjustment should be during the engagement, and that the marriage should be "merely a matter of rounding off the rough edges." Number six, showing a little more hostility, I shall quote in full: "The biggest adjustment is getting used to another person handling the money you worked for. Things are rosy at the start when both people are working. The real test starts with the first baby, when only one pay-check is brought home. And then there isn't enough cash so the wife goes credit card crazy." The seventh replied that money management is the biggest adjustment, comparing the difference between doing pretty much as one pleased before marriage with the necessity now of facing fixed charges and living within a budget. The last man said, "If you stay as self-centered as you were in single life your marriage is doomed. It need not be a prison. You enjoy finding out what she wants. And one important point is to do things together. No nights out with the boys. That's the beginning of trouble."

If these replies were to be read to a group of a half-dozen married couples, an interesting discussion might be provoked! Money was specifically mentioned by four out of eight and implied by two others. The suggestion that marriage means a loss of independence is a steady note and one reporter goes out of his way to say that marriage is not a "prison." In several of the responses one gets a whiff of the eternal male-female warfare celebrated by the late James Thurber. (Any couple contemplating marriage, either before or after the event, should read *The Unicorn in the Garden*.) Since money seems to be one of the major causes of friction let us start with that.

Money, Money, Money

The trouble with money is that nobody has enough of it until he comes to the point where he doesn't need it. That is to say that money, like sex, is a power symbol. We need the money as long as we need the power, and everything in our culture pattern tells us loudly that we need the power. Children dream up and share with close friends extravagant fancies of what they would do if they had a million dollars, and the fancies are of course ego-extensions: a castle, a yacht, a space ship. There is a TV show turning upon the same dream: a person is given a check for a million dollars, by some miracle tax-free, and told to spend it. I can remember being captivated as a child, as many others have been before and since, by the magic of Alexandre Dumas' Count of Monte Cristo who, having learned several languages and the wisdom of the ages in prison, finds the hidden inexhaustible treasure and with a limitless future bestrides the world, "monarch of all I survey." But for most of us such imaginings are just that. Our problem is how to pay the grocery bill. Or, to change the figure but not the reality, one of the characters in George Santayana's *The Last Puritan*, a down to earth woman, remarks to Mr. Oliver that we seem to be able to endure great sorrows since they are a part of our common humanity. They even lend a dignity to our lives and give us a little importance. What she worries about is the price of eggs.

Most of us get along without a million dollars; what we want is *enough* money. Enough for what? Well, enough to pay the bills and educate the children and do a few interesting things. Then the question intrudes, What makes things interesting? I have watched sad people, bound by invisible strings to slot machines in places like Reno, who do not appear to find life very interesting. Many get caught in the upward spiral of keeping up with the Joneses, and a new science has grown up among us which investigates the reasons why people buy the things they buy. Some of this is fascinating, much of it is amusing. George Ade, the Will Rogers of his day, observed that people should live within their income even if they had to borrow the money to do it! A little car will get us where we want to go as well as a big one, but it will not make our neighbors sick with envy. Perhaps that is a desirable end; it would appear that many think so. Old furniture is usually more comfortable than new furniture, and people who have new clothes can afford to wear old ones. Most Americans at the moment have more things than they need, a fact we discover when we come to move.

Let us go back to the couple starting out on their matrimonial adventure. They have some clothes and other personal belongings, some wedding presents, perhaps some unpaid bills, and a job. If the man is a graduate student, it may be the girl who has the job. As soon as they have a street address they will begin to receive mail from the local stores describing things they will surely want to have. It seems easy to buy things when they cost so little each month and are so attractive. But one needs a priority list. In Chapter 2 ("Problems") I tried to put the four questions about money in order of appearance: total income, debts and immediate expenses, budget, financial responsibilities beyond the local family circle. Hopefully, total income will have been discussed before the marriage begins, and in advance it usually looks adequate. There are always extras on the second item. A general law of nature seems to be: whatever it is, it takes longer and costs more. The budget question, though, is where we get down to brass tacks. So much comes in as salary or whatever; so much goes out in fixed charges like rent; so much is estimated for necessities like food. The hope, of course, is that the expenses will be less than the income and perhaps leave a small balance for savings and emergencies.

This is a matter partly, but not entirely, of arithmetic. You will remember that in the sidewalk interviews the question of money was closely bound up with loss of independence, conflicting interests, and the question of who does the spending. If a budget is agreed upon and one of the marriage partners goes out of bounds, putting an unexpected strain on the economy, a lot more than money is involved. If this happens frequently, it can get pretty discouraging. Joint accounts are a good thing as long as the marriage is joint. If a husband and wife represent different schools of thought on toothpaste-squeezing, they might solve the problem by buying two tubes of it; but if money which has been counted on disappears week after week, or month after month, the marriage is in trouble. Some men feel that their masculinity is threatened if they do not keep the family books, even if they do so quite badly. I have no idea what the statistics are on this matter but it would seem to me that the family financier ought to be the person who can do it best, with the least fuss and the most harmony. The Victorian husband retired to his study in Olympian detachment and did the accounts. It was assumed that his wife could not add two and two and come up with four. Sometimes it was true that she could not, not because she was a woman but because she had not learned. It was not her place. Now there are prophets among us who tell us that the American woman is about to take over everything. Again, we might remember that a man does not marry the American woman; he married this very girl because he loved her, and she might be very good at keeping the family books. Together they might figure out what they can afford to spend separately without guilt and what they prefer to spend doing things together. The nostalgic fancy of the man for his single days, when his pockets jingled, has a parallel in the romantic dream of the Monte Cristo millionaire who owns half of the world and would rather have a hearth and home of his own, with all its problems.

Separate Interests

Divided interests, unshared, sometimes cause trouble. The golf widow and the bridge widower are familiar figures. There is no reason why a man should not play golf with men friends or why a woman should not play bridge with women friends, or the other way around. The deadly thing for a marriage is the grooves: *every* afternoon at bridge, *every* Saturday at the golf course. Every marriage needs some privacy, some room for special interests, some breathing spaces. But the end of it is to come together again richer than before. Once the grooves are hardened the marriage tends to run in them. A rather extreme symbol of this comes to mind. There were two sisters I once knew in New England who shared an apartment in the winter and a house near the sea in the summer. The seashore house was fascinating because it was divided into two halves like a stage set. One sister loved to paint, kept a delightfully casual house, or half a house, cluttered with paint pots, unfinished pictures and painting gear of all kinds, shapes and smells. She was usually to be found in a painty smock, ancient tennis shoes and a floppy hat. She practically lived in the kitchen where she slept on a cot under a window with a view. She had an untidy dog who sometimes changed color in spots. The other half of the house looked like a set for *Life with Father*—very prim and proper, highly polished and well dusted. There was a place for everything and it was there. This sister dressed severely, did beautiful cross-stitch work, slept in a bed in a bedroom, and kept a stately cat. The divided house did not represent a feud, at least not now, but a living arrangement. One enjoyed both sides very much but called on them separately. The sisters visited each other by invitation. For their purposes it was a sensible enough arrangement and seemed to work quite well. But the walls of partition clearly defined separate lives. Separate interests are a blessing to a marriage if they can be brought home to the same hearth, even if only with a smile of recognition and some understanding that the other enjoys what he or she is doing. It is then a pleasure for both.

In the early days of the marriage everything possible is done together. It is part of the delight in being married. What he wants to do is what she wants to do, whether she had planned it that way or not. And it is equally true the other way. There may be a twinge of guilt when separate interests and activities begin to appear some time later. This is the meeting place or the dividing place. From here the paths may diverge until there are hills and valleys between them, sometimes impassable, or the landscape may be viewed differently or a different landscape viewed, but from the same path. The path may be a broad one with opportunities for different pace, and different things may catch the eye or engage the hand, but there are meeting places where the travelers may sit down and talk about what they have seen.

Fatigue

No one works well, plays well, or thinks well when he is tired. Some interesting studies have been made recently in the armed forces on the subject of fatigue and efficiency. They tend to prove through scientific testing what we have always known; but the ratio between fatigue and loss of efficiency appears to be much higher than many of us would have guessed. Our old companion fatigue assumes many familiar attitudes. A man may get up tired after a bad night, find himself disorganized, his fingers all thumbs, his brain numb. He struggles through the day somehow, weighing twice as much as he should, finally gets home to find the pleasantly disorganized atmosphere of the house almost more than he can bear. Words are spoken, and replied to. There is a small scene which bothers and mystifies the children, and the evening ahead is already in shreds. Or there may come a day when the wife feels that she simply cannot get out of bed and start the thing all over again. Not today. Life must have been meant to be better than this old treadmill. Live happily ever after. Ha! When do we start? Once again the day is lived through, but it is about three days long. Any chance for a nap was ruined by the telephone and a vacuum cleaner salesman. The children are monsters. By the time her husband comes home she could eat him in two bites, for no other reason except that there he is!

Any people not recently married, who happen to be reading these words, will know that the problem is not so much with one bad night followed by a bad day as it is all the days followed by all the nights followed by all the days. Almost anybody can live through a crisis and do pretty well, but the accumulated tiredness of the daily attrition can enter into the bones. There is no solution to this problem; there are some helps, however. Let us begin with the worst, the homecoming. Earlier I mentioned that a friend of mine had learned to pray on the commuting train. There is a starting place. All prayer begins with attention and attention needs repose. With a little practice one can learn to compose himself almost anywhere. But it has to be *done*, not just thought about. It requires a gentle but firm act of the will. Five minutes upstairs if the children are down, or downstairs if they are up; five minutes behind a protecting newspaper on the commuting train with one's eyes closed, or while walking a familiar street with one's eyes open but the eye of the mind focused elsewhere. Begin with the Lord's Prayer, slowly, remembering your husband or wife by name with each phrase. At the end of it ask God's blessing on your home and children, your marriage, the day's work, the things done and left undone. By now you will have calmed down, you may even be smiling. No magic, just the goodness of God.

A number of married people I know have revived an old custom for this time of day, the custom of tea. It sounds a bit quaint, yet it is immensely practical. Consider the alternatives. One of them is nothing at all except the chance or hope that somehow things will be all right. There are those times, of course, when for no assignable reason one feels just fine, rested and mellow and interested in what is going on. But they cannot easily be anticipated. Another alternative is the cocktail hour. This often serves a good purpose. It may be an end of the day glass of beer or sherry instead of a martini, but the real point of it is the pause, the resting place where two paths meet. The advantage some find with tea is that it actually is a pick-up, a genuine stimulant, that it does not put one to sleep, that it costs less, that at the end of two or three cups one can still hear what the other is saying. But again, the important point is the pause, the meeting, the chance to put two days back into one day.

And then, the Children

We have already thought some about children. There are two kinds of children trouble. One is the series of crises married people somehow live through: the cuts and bruises, the serious falls and broken bones, the sudden sickness with fever soaring in the middle of the night, the hot face on the white pillow, the epidemic when everybody has it. It sometimes seems a wonder that anyone lives to grow up. But we do, and all of it is a part of the family history forever. The other sort of children trouble is more serious but often as unpredictable. I am thinking of the child who goes wrong, who for no reason that the average parent can understand refuses friendship at home and finds his associations in another place. We know more about these things than we once did and we are grateful for the resources now open to us. But it is often a heartbreak for the parents, who need the love and understanding and support of their friends.

Sometimes so much happens so fast or so often that it just doesn't matter any more. A widow was left with two lively daughters to bring up. She was a resourceful person and a good mother; but no one could have kept up with the capacity of the older girl for getting into trouble. And of all kinds. It was genius. If a window was broken in the neighborhood, it was Janet who broke it. If only one person in a class of forty got scarlet fever, it was Janet. If a child rolled off the living room couch and broke her arm, you could know before you looked that it was Janet. One evening, just as the girl's mother was putting supper on the table, the telephone rang. It was the police. "I am sorry to tell you," the voice said, "that we have just picked up your daughter Janet with a broken leg and have taken her to the hospital." "What?" replied the mother wearily, "only *one* broken leg?"

Many of the troubles we live through in families are fondly remembered for years once they are safely in the past. Some of these are little things, as a child telling the awful truth in a piping voice at some really awkward moment. It has been observed that children under ten and women over seventy tell the truth—plain, straight, and unvarnished. In neither case is there any reason to conceal it. If the truth is what you want, this is the place to go. But it can be devastating when offered unexpectedly. Another fondly remembered time, and often retold, is the time when everything went wrong: the dinner burned, and the pie dropped face down, and there was a distinguished guest.

Troublemakers

There are a number of ways not to meet trouble in a marriage. We might give titles to some of the old regulars. For example, The Hot Retort. This is always a temptation, especially if one is clever at it. The satisfaction of ending an encounter with one masterly withering phrase is one which dies hard in us. There is a famous story of a professor in a theological school criticizing a sermon which a young man had slaved over for hours. At the end of it the professor said caustically, "That sermon is much too long. You could throw half of it away, and it wouldn't matter which half." Without doubt a clever remark, and one which has been retold for years. But one wonders about the young man whose name nobody remembers. What happened to him? There is another clue here. The acid of sarcasm always leaves a scar. The professor quoted just now may have said many helpful things to many students, doubtless did, but the rapier thrust is the remembered one. When a wife, moved to anger, blazes at her husband, "If you're such a big shot, why don't you fire the boss and take his job?", it is likely to be remembered. When a husband in an unwise moment flings at his wife, "If all your brains blew up at once it wouldn't muss your hair," it is likely to be remembered. The Hot Retort is emotionally expensive. Few can afford it. Swallow hard and don't say it. A young couple had their first big row during their honeymoon at a little place in Switzerland called Sollochs. The battle was resolved (some of our fondest memories of loving moments are of those after a row) and the couple decided that in the future whenever an emotional storm threatened and the hot words were about to be said, one or the other of them would say "Sollochs," and there would follow a five minute silence. There is a great difference between a battle which may clear the air, may even be enjoyable for its own sake, and the branding iron of sarcasm. Friction sometimes produces sparks which are illuminating, sarcasm only wounds and leaves a mark.

The Cold Sulk. This is a little harder to deal with than the hot word because it retreats into silence and sullenness. It has a mouth. Usually the person sulking can be drawn out of it by being agreed with or flattered; but it isn't always worth it. The sulk is a weapon commonly used by young women to get their own way. Since it thrives on audience response, it can perhaps be best countered by the lack of it. While a person who sulks frequently is not grown up enough to be married, she may be worth waiting out.

The Deep Freeze is more serious because it retreats farther, is less accessible. This is cold hostility, tight-lipped and distant as a star. It is sometimes used as a punishment for some real or fancied wrong, and in this respect is about as ineffective as most methods of punishment. Presumably, after one marriage partner has been kept in the freezer for a sufficient length of time, he or she is supposed to emerge benefited by the experience, though it is difficult to understand why. The person doing the freezing refuses to talk so it is not much help if the other person wishes to. This is a prideful sort of thing that drains the love out of a marriage and sterilizes the ground where it might grow again.

The Wounded Martyr. This is very satisfying because it

has not only gestures and postures; it has speeches! It sounds like the comic cards one finds in railroad stations and airports: I gave you the best years of my life and what did I get out of it? The bills. The Wounded Martyr must be treated with care because he or she is very tender at the time the martyrdom is being expressed. All is saved if the martyr can laugh at himself, but to be laughed at would simply increase his sense of being wronged, or at least of being unappreciated. "Don't worry about me, I'll be all right," says the wounded male. "Well, I guess I just haven't known how to make you happy; goodness knows I've tried hard enough," says the wounded female.

Then there is The Righteous One. This person has a self-bestowed honorary degree in rightness. He walks taller than his fellow plodders and breathes the lofty air of High Principle. He knows his duty and he frequently feels the responsibility of pointing out others' duty to them. I once listened to a man while he complained at some length about his wife's conduct. They had been married about ten years, there were no children, and he was about to leave. The three of us spent a long evening together in the course of which I asked him if during his life he had ever done anything which he would consider wrong. He thought about it briefly, then said simply that he had not. Most Righteous Ones do not reach such a height, but there is always that unmistakable superiority above the common herd. Mark Twain tells of a man who was so proud he expected to be foreman of the jury on the Day of Judgment.

Long before now you will have seen the point of these caricatures. Each of us is partly all five of these poses and, from time to time, more one than another. The fact is that we are all funny, ridiculous; the trouble is that we forget it.

It seems unsurprising to us that other people should be hot retorters, or cold sulkers, or wounded martyrs; after all they are just people while we are different. All of *our* complaints are real, our descriptions accurate, our hurt feelings justified. It takes a while for people, married or unmarried, to get over feeling like the innocent party. It may be true that married people have more provocation since they are at closer quarters with at least one other human being. I am not sure; there are other quarters which can be very close. But it is true that married people have the possibility of a community, with love and understanding for solvents, in a relationship which is peculiar to itself.

Enough Wisdom . . . with Love

Anyone having persevered thus far in this book will be sure, I hope, that I do not believe in ideal marriages any more than I believe in ideal people. I believe in real people with real problems and real lives to live, some of whom have joined themselves together in Christian marriage. A Christian may be a number of things, but he has no right to be astonished either by the frailty of human nature or the goodness of God. In this light a Christian and his wife may learn enough wisdom so they can smile at themselves and therefore at each other, with love.

We do well to remember that all families live double lives. There is the group life which our friends and neighbors observe, which is caught for a second artificially in the unblinking eye of a camera before it moves off again into its infinitely complicated relationships. But for each member of this family group there is a desperate struggle for his individual survival. It begins the day he is born. Sometimes this struggle comes into view, as in our caricatures, more often it is concealed. But it is there all the time. Each of us is vulnerable, each of us fighting for his life, each of us trying to break out of a net which circumstances and our own affections have woven about us. No human relationship can be perfect because half of us is running toward it and the other half trying to escape from it.

There are times when we find ourselves in deep waters and need more and different help than common sense can give us. Then we turn to our friend the psychiatrist, the marriage counselor, the skillful pastor. Meanwhile, we have a partnership in our trouble, a person with whom we can talk about it. And that is the beginning of the "solving" of it; not in a static sense like a puzzle but in a dynamic sense with human beings, under God, laughing and crying, reaching out and drawing back, living under a roof, walking up a road, raising up children, stifling fears and sharing unexpected joys.

11 · Why Marriages Break

A MARRIAGE BREAKS WHEN THERE IS NOT ENOUGH TO HOLD IT together, and when some event or series of events brings this fact to the inescapable attention of one or both of the marriage partners. It is not ordinarily a sudden thing so much as a gradual disintegration of the relationship, or a gradual disclosure that there was not enough in common in the first place. Approximately one half of the divorces in this country are granted to couples who have been married less than six years. It is not uncommon for a couple to meet on the basis of a strong physical attraction and to get married on the strength of it, only to find that it does not last when there is nothing much for it to speak for. There is not enough building material to make a house. But many couples simply do not give themselves enough time to work through the necessary adjustment and integration of two human beings living together for the first time. Also, since the current trend is to marry younger, it is not surprising that many young people have not made up their own minds about important issues and concerns, to say nothing about their unreadiness to share what views they do have as offerings and not bulwarks to crouch behind or platforms on which to stand while talking. And, inevitably, many of these points of view will reflect those of other people taken over in undigested chunks. On the other hand young couples who are secure in enough common ground on which to build, and who are open and undefensive with each other, have the pleasure of growing up together and in good sense educating one another.

Every marriage has its bad moments and people who have been married for twenty years or more can look back on a patchwork quilt of days and years. There were times when, with one more push or one less defense, the house might have fallen apart. Little divorces and reconciliations take place frequently in marriage. This is the alternative to the romantic myth of living happily ever after with no problems of any kind. In a real marriage one remembers old differences and difficulties with a gentle affection—"that's how I know it's George." But this takes some winning, and the perspective of distance. It is a good thing, a very good thing, which young couples may anticipate with joy, but it cannot be won in a night nor produced artificially. Actually the raw material for lasting marriages and broken ones is about the same. The difference is in how it is used.

Two Scenes

We might look in at a couple between one and five years out when they are at odds, to see what elements are there. Let us call them John and Mary, for convenience. Scene One discloses Mary in the kitchen. She is singing while she does the supper dishes when John saunters out to help. He picks up a glass to dry it but Mary takes it out of his hand and puts it back in the drainer. "They haven't been rinsed yet," she explains patiently as to a child. "Well, for goodness sake, why don't you rinse them under the tap as you wash them?" And the material for the battle is there. It is surprising what a hidden minefield a kitchen can be. In no time at all we have three possible sets of disagreement. One is the way I was brought up *versus* the way you were brought up or, more precisely, my mother *versus* your mother. The second is two conflicting, equally defensible schools of thought on dish-washing, each represented by a local champion. And thirdly, the matter of conflicting roles. "After all," says the husband in an aggrieved tone, "I just came out to help and all this happened." "Well," replies the wife, "whose kitchen is it anyway?" Whose indeed? This skirmish is revealing, but so is its aftermath. What happens now? John may entrench himself in silence behind a newspaper, or he may leave the house with or without saying some things which he will later regret having said. Mary may burst into tears or she may harden her heart. But the real question is, will they talk about it or will they bury it and make believe that it did not happen. If they can talk about it sometime soon when they are calm, either coming to some simple working agreement or really agreeing that it is not important, they may still be married some years later. If they push it down in silence it will remain a hard lump of unresolved hostility to be added to other lumps and plague them later. The incident needs an apology, on both sides, but a gentle one. A stiff apology is a second insult. The injured party—in this case two of them—does not want to be compensated because he was wronged; he wants to be healed because he was hurt. And more, no one can heal either of these persons of this particular hurt except the other one.

Let us look at Scene Two. John and Mary are having

breakfast. It is the usual early morning hurry with John gulping coffee as he glances at the headlines and the clock. Mary is not looking quite her best as she deals with John and the children, and the toaster which has never worked properly. The radio is blaring cheerfully in a brassy voice, interrupted by a brief news bulletin that the world is going to pot. After some poking and prying Mary reports that the toaster has this time finally given up the struggle. John is piqued.

"What? No toast? Why didn't you get the thing fixed?" The implication is that time hangs heavy on her hands all day long. She bristles.

"I asked you to fix it last Saturday but you were too busy watching the ball game." The children make breakfast noises while husband and wife glare at each other.

"It seems to me," says John loftily, "that you could be responsible for the operation of the kitchen, if that is not expecting too much."

"So speaks the lordly male! Well, let me tell you something, John Brooks."

"Oh to hell with it," says John as, darting a look at the clock, he slams out the door and starts the car.

A cold wind blows through the room.

After the children are shushed and variously dealt with Mary may do a number of things. She may cry, she may call her mother or some other woman and discuss men and their shortcomings. She may just stare at the wall and wonder what happened to the good years. John arriving at his place of work, looking both hurt and angry, may tell his tale and receive comfort. Or he may just stare at his desk and wonder what happened to the good years.

These illustrations are overbrief and overstated, but perhaps we can use them as source material for recognizing some of the danger signals in a marriage. Obviously there are many kitchens which do not explode when a couple join forces for dish-washing. Many wives would be surprised to see their husbands in the kitchen at all at such a time, and according to some observers they would be better off alone. Similarly, numbers of people survive the death of the toaster without such stormy results. But nevertheless, while we are inquiring into the causes of marriage failures, here are some of the makings.

The Power of Words

From early childhood boys and girls are taught the virtues of team-play, a point of view which is adopted with some reluctance. Perhaps the most characteristic remark of any child, as displaying his human nature is, "Hey Ma, look at me!" This is natural man, unadorned and undisguised. We grow more subtle after a while and display our charms and our accomplishments with more artistry. But the will to win is still there and still strong. If it were not so we would probably not grow old enough to be married. The operating question is, winning at whose expense? We thought of The Righteous One whose burden in life is to be always Right, and in his case at the expense of *everyone* else. Some of this attitude persists in all of us and we shall die with it. We know that children learn with difficulty that other people have opinions and privileges and are persons in their own right. It may be hoped that, by the time the same children reach the marrying age, this lesson will have been learned well enough so that another human being can be seen as an end in himself. We considered this approach some time ago in regard to respect. Without it any marriage is in for a bad time, perhaps failure. Pride and hostility are old friends. In the morality plays of the middle ages such qualities were personified. In our time the device has been revived by several poets and dramatists, the late Charles Williams for example, in *Grab and Grace* and *The House by the Stable*. It is a helpful literary use since we do choose most of our companions. Hostility is in all of us, in the sense in which all men are enemies, but it can be cultivated or minimized. When we cultivate it, we are by way of becoming Right and venting our spleen. We like to think of it as "righteous indignation." It seems a good excuse for being angry, which is always self-defeating. By the time we stand before the altar and say the committing words, our thankfulness for the gift of love should have absorbed, or can begin to absorb, the cold superiority of pride and the stabbing thrust of anger. The marriage is, in Jeremy Taylor's good phrase, a "school of charity" or it is a jungle place where creatures devour one another. Usually it is some of both. The problem for a man and woman moving toward maturity is to discover ways to charity while recognizing the jungle and making as little as possible of it. We shall think more about this.

The Romans had a proverb, they liked proverbs, "The spoken word perishes, the written word remains." As in the case of many proverbs it is only half true. Written words do have a long life—sometimes embarrassingly so—but so do spoken words. One of the earliest memories of any person is of words spoken to him or in his presence. Words long ago forgotten by the speaker may live a lifetime in the memory of another person and perhaps be passed along in the oral tradition to another generation. Some phrases and slogans seem to be timeless and have played influential roles in the affairs of men and nations. So with marriages. A man and woman will remember all their lives the words one or both of them said on some of their historic occasions. Perhaps they will be able to recall what they talked about at their first meeting, or the words of proposal and acceptance. Sometimes a remark occasioned by some particular incident will become a family byword and will come to represent an attitude about life in general. The astonishing thing about words is how many of them are remembered, especially when spoken in times of emotional involvement. Words of love will be remembered—so will words of hate, of fear, of anxiety. In times of marriage difficulties when people are angry and feel threatened they are likely to say too much, both in attack and defense. Sometimes the words are regretted as soon as they are out, but it is too late to get them back. It is not uncommon in the course of a criminal trial for a witness to make a fiery statement of opinion which the presiding judge will rule out of order, instructing the members of the jury to disregard it. They may perhaps be able to do so when weighing up the evidence but chances are that words so spoken will have their influence, consciously or unconsciously, on the minds of the hearers. And so it is when a man and his wife are for a moment more enemies than friends. The words are weapons and they are meant to wound or kill. Sometimes they do. There is a secret line which is crossed after which it is difficult or impossible to cross back again. An incident occurs, usually something rather unimportant in itself, but it represents a deeper difference. Pride is invoked. This time he will stand his ground; this time she will not give in as she has all too often. Anger is kindled and defense quickly shifts to attack. The silly little fracas is used as a symbol of any differences the couple have ever had. It may work up to such words as, "Well, if that's the way you feel about it . . . ," met by, "That is precisely the way I feel about it." Something has been hurt, twisted. Usually then the antagonists seek out friends to agree that they have been dealt with outrageously. This is not so bad, may even be a safety valve. Couples sometimes threaten each other with the possibility of divorce. And the line is really crossed when one of them goes to a lawyer about it. This is a different sort of third party and while reconciliations do take place at the last minute, the invoking of the law has a finality about it.

The Death of Love

Long before this time these people may have come to the point where they can no longer talk to each other without having a storm blow up. They simply articulate their hostilities and incompatibilities, their dissatisfactions with one another, no matter what the subject matter of the argument may be. Or they may discover that it has been years since they have talked about anything that really matters and now they have nothing to talk about. The marriage has quietly died under them and it is too late to revive it. The living arrangement may continue for any one of a number of reasons; but the marriage is over. To be widowed by the death of love can be sadder than to be widowed by the death of the body. A marriage can drift apart gradually, the partners finding friendship outside of it, taking affection within it for granted until they discover one day that it is not there any more, perhaps has not been for a long time. It is possible to fall out of love as well as to fall into it. Perhaps one was more in love with the idea of being in love than with any particular agent of it. It does happen. But for whatever reason, the marriage is dead. And if this is true it will probably stay dead.

Tightly, with Open Hands

Sometimes marriages die because they are held too tightly, squeezed to death. A young woman married four or five years writes, "John and I have been becoming friends this year because he can share himself with me sometimes and I can let him go sometimes." Any human relationship can be choked by over-possessiveness. A woman can ask a man too many times if he loves her. Reconsidering the question one of these days he may discover that he does not. It is well to hold tightly with open hands. Ambrose Bierce once said, "Oh, that we could fall into woman's arms without falling into her hands." One of the most delightful unpossessive stories I know has to do with a charming woman married to a college professor at a women's college. They were a hospitable pair and enjoyed the company and conversation of students in their comfortable home. During a summer session a group of a dozen or so had dropped in to listen to music and talk. It was a warm evening, windows wide open and a general feeling of informality, most of the girls sitting on the floor. One attractive student seemed bent upon getting through to the professor, almost as if she had made a bet that she could do so. He became aware of her attention and also of the fact that she had very little on. He reacted moderately, walked to another place in the living room and sat down to talk with someone else. In no time at all his pursuer was there too, sitting at his feet looking up and displaying her charms which were considerable. The man glanced at his wife. No sign was flashed, though he did notice a small curly smile as she sewed and talked with the girls on either side of her. Presently the telephone rang and the professor escaped to the hall to answer it. When he came back the girl was lying in the doorway so he had to step over her to enter the room. She looked up at him and smiled. A few minutes later the man and his wife passed each other in the hall, busy with refreshments. As they passed she winked and whispered, "How are you doing?" Holding with open hands indeed!

Indices of Maturity

Many marriages, like other things, break for lack of support. I am not thinking now only of financial support, though that is important as we all know. I am thinking of emotional support. As in one's religious life it comes in two categories, public and private. At a social gathering recently I watched a man support his rather shy wife skillfully and unobtrusively. He was attractive and quick-witted and it would have been easy for him to have been the life of the party without half trying and to have gone home socially victorious. In my estimate he did indeed do so but in a better sense than that of personal victory. He did not occupy all of the spotlight or insist on telling all of the stories. Smoothly and with no suggestion of, "Now it's your turn, dear," the conversation was made a double one and two well-married people went home having supported each other pleasantly and enjoyably in public. The opposite of this is the destruction of being criticized in public for a fault or failing learned in private. There is no more effective way to destroy a marriage. Private support comes in all the ways, secret and open, in which a man and his wife minister to each other. It begins with listening and really hearing, with looking and really seeing; and it goes on from there to the healing of understanding and the warmth of love. It is the opposite of the strained or blank married silence where two people sit in a room as if they had not yet been introduced to each other.

There is no such thing as a marriage which is compatible all the time. It is an achievement when a marriage is compatible most of the time, which means that the members of it have worked out a living arrangement in which creative interchange can take place and destruction be kept at a minimum. Like any friendship a marriage has to be kept in repair. It is good to settle differences when they are still little ones, before they become larger than they have any right to be and blot out the sun. Married couples have different ways of handling this. Some set aside a time each week, Sunday night perhaps, for a sort of review of events and reactions. Others prefer to do so more informally. But the real point is that such a meeting takes place one way or another and that this man and this woman can begin to practice speaking freely and honestly about real things. I have suggested an index of maturity—the manner in which a person endures monotony. I shall now suggest another —the willingness to accept criticism, in private, from a husband or a wife.

If They Can Continue to Meet . . .

There is often quite a difference between real and alleged causes of divorce and not all alleged causes are simply convenient fictions; sometimes the divorcing parties are not aware of the real causes themselves. Anyone old enough to be reading this book knows the big words which are the grounds on which most divorces are granted in the United States: cruelty, desertion, adultery, neglect to provide, drunkenness. About nine out of every ten of all the divorces in our country are granted on one or another of these grounds. But that does not really say very much. What caused the "cruelty"? Why did she leave him, or he her? Why was there room or necessity for another sexual partner? Why did the husband or wife spiral into drunkenness? The answers to these questions, if they could be found, might help any couple to understand the nature of their own unrelatedness and perhaps to find one another again. I suppose that at no period in history up to our own time has so much thought and research been spent on such questions. Much new light has been shed, for which we are grateful. But the answers, I think, are to be found, if they are to be found at all, not so much by compiling statistics, however painstakingly, as through a deepened understanding of men and women and their needs. Some of the present studies are in this direction. We have thought about our need to be noticed, wanted, loved, respected, used, completed. We have considered that our love for one another, always conditional and always partly selfish, is a pale reflection of the unconditional and almost unbelievable love of God for us. We have thought that if our religion is to be real that it must be practised. We have thought about the mystery of meeting and about some of the forms of competition which destroy community. In the midst of all of these concerns, tensions, and speculations are two human beings, a man and a woman, who met and fell in love and had great hopes. If they can continue to meet in their bodies, in their prayers, and in their conversation they can survive almost anything and build a home.

There is an interesting difference in how men and women think about each other before and after marriage. Before marriage men, following the romantic pattern, often idealize their women, and after marriage sometimes idealize other women. The situation can remain idealized, and nourishing to an artistic temperament, as long as it does not become anything else. People have speculated on what might have happened if Dante had married Beatrice. He saw her only once, you may recall, walking with two other girls on a street in Florence. He was some years her senior and after her death did himself marry; but the sight of her, and what to Dante was her unearthly beauty, lasted him all his life. She became his angel, his guide, his beatitude. The situation would doubtless have been quite different had she presided over his bed and board instead of his creative imagination, and perhaps to the poverty of all of us. Here is a small piece of the puzzle of human relationships; a man needs an angel but not to marry. Any woman would rather be a woman than an angel, but so also would she rather be partly an angel than entirely a short-order cook. She has to settle for a multiple role.

A woman inside a marriage looking out at other women in *their* various roles is apt to be both distrustful and protective. In a delightfully pungent book called *The Influence of Women and Its Cure,*° written twenty-five years ago, John Erskine said:

". . . Women never trust each other. They won't admit

° Copyright 1936 by John Erskine and used by special permission of the publishers, The Bobbs-Merrill Company, Inc.

that they themselves are acquisitive or possessive where an outstanding man is concerned, but they see clearly that every other woman is. In your wife's opinion her initial interest in you was a harmony of spirit, ordained in heaven, but the admiration of other women is just an index of their low character—and yours. For you to attract her was beautiful; for you to be attracted to them is treacherous."

Can a woman love two men at the same time? Can a man love two women at the same time? The question has never been answered satisfactorily, and I am certainly not going to attempt it here. Meanings overlap, and we are born with a clever ability to make things come out the way we want them to. Holding with open hands is the nearest I can come to an answer.

Good Fridays and Easters

It would be dishonest and sentimental not to admit that there are marriages which should not continue. Some marriages contracted in haste without the necessary consideration or without sufficient preparation simply do not have enough to go on, and no amount of good will or skillful counseling after the fact can make up for the lack. And we have already noted that a marriage does not become a Christian union just because the couple were married in a Christian church or by a Christian minister. In many cases the intention of a Christian marriage is not involved and the resources of the Church are therefore irrelevant. Countless couples, both inside and outside the Church, have never experienced holy matrimony and should not be judged as religiously responsible. There are marriages which from the outset seem to contain elements destructive to its fabric, marriages which should not have been contracted. Sometimes there are physical or emotional or psychological conditions which make the marriage impossible of fulfillment. Various church bodies will deal with such cases according to their beliefs and their experience. Church bodies, such as the Episcopal Church, which are governed by canon law make their own definitions of fact and possibility; and these are plain for the world to read and know. Decisions in such situations are serious responsibilities and are taken seriously. Divorce is as old as marriage and there is no culture on record which does not recognize some set of circumstances which make the annulment or the dissolution of a marriage permissible. Many psychiatrists would argue that the nature of the offense has little or nothing to do with the need for divorce. What does matter, they would say, is the attitude of the marriage partners toward their own marriage. Christians, by and large, would agree with this, adding that in a Christian marriage the attitude of the partners is a part of their attitude as Christians to the whole spectrum of life and living.

Christians who marry have more and better resources than the world knows, as we have seen in earlier chapters, principally 4 and 5. But the fact remains that there are cases when all the resources in the world do not seem adequate to the need or, more precisely perhaps, when such resources cannot be accepted and used. There are cases which a responsible church body can declare never were Christian marriages and are subject to annulment or dissolution. In such instances the parties, or sometimes one of them, are eligible for remarriage under church auspices. And the record for the success of such remarriages is generally good.

It is the belief of a number of Christian marriage counselors that couples whose marriages are seriously threatened cannot be helped much pastorally unless they are willing to consider the possibility of terminating their marriage. Some of the difficulty here reflects both the inadequacy of preparation for holy matrimony and the pastoral irresponsibility of clergymen who marry couples merely because they appear on the doorstep and ask for it. Only committed Christians can pretend to enter into holy matrimony and to stay in that state.

Life is filled with little deaths and little resurrections, minor tragedies and minor ecstasies. Many marriages know their own Good Fridays when there is darkness over all the earth, and many have survived the dark time, by the grace of God and the practical assistance of godly helpers, to know also their own Easter.

12 · Reconciliation

RECONCILIATION IS A TALL WORD. IT DOES NOT MEAN SIMPLY that hostilities have ceased, that there is a truce. It means that enemies have become friends again, that forgiveness and restoration have taken place. It is a new creature. It is a rising from the dead. It is a miracle of love soaking up and blotting out a season of hatred and fear. And it is costly.

Lovers' quarrels are real enough, usually brief and intense, sometimes very satisfying in their resolution. But they are early in the marriage or even previous to it. They represent no more than two young people trying to find themselves and their relationship to each other. There is not yet much to fight over because there has not been a lot of emotional investment. The walls of the house have not cracked; they are bickering about what color to paint the front door. When the deep trouble comes, it has to be met deeply. Ordinarily we human beings like to put off as long as possible any negative truth about ourselves. When we have a toothache, we postpone as long as we can the moment when we actually pick up the telephone and call the dentist. We hope that in some magical way the pain will change its mind and go away if we pay no attention to it. Sometimes it does, but whatever caused it is probably still there and after a while will make itself known again. We have reminded ourselves that little hurts and disagreements left unresolved tend to grow in size and importance. We know this but, as with the dentist, we put off doing anything about it. This is true partly because if the issue is faced head-on it will have to be recognized as at least one person's fault, if not more, and changes may have to be made. And if there is one thing which we resist even more than facing negative truth about ourselves it is doing anything about it. We resist change in general, but especially when it involves our personal habits and attitudes. Then our defenses come up and each of us tends to be Right.

When this has gone on long enough there are two camps instead of one house and, between the camps, a war. Once the bitter words have been said and the lines of battle drawn, are there ways to peace, to a new beginning? There are, but they are not easy. The hardest for most people is the one we have just been considering—willingness to discuss the situation at all in any terms other than accusations. There is a law of nature as deep as any that no situation, personal or social, can be changed in any direction until it is accepted the way it is. We know this in our minds but we resist it with our emotions. Let me illustrate. Once there was a woman who wanted to kill her husband—symbolically in this case, but in her heart she wanted him dead. They had been married a dozen years and had one child, a girl now eleven. The wife was not the easiest person in the world to live with. She was not young when she married and she had all the raw material for being a shrew: a sharp nose, an angular body, gimlety eyes behind rimless spectacles, a habit of complaining about everything in a voice with a good cutting edge. Her husband was a fisherman out of a New England port, an easygoing fellow who stayed away from home as long and as often as possible, though he missed the girl. They had always enjoyed each other's company, partly as an unspoken alliance against mother. After a particularly stormy period at home the husband put to sea again, having made certain small preparations, determined not to come back again, ever. When the vessel, a large one, stopped at a port city several hundred miles away, the man—we might call him Harry—put his sea bag on his shoulder and walked ashore feeling more relieved than he had felt in years. He got a job in a navy yard and his new life began.

When Harry did not come home with the ship, Clara, his wife, made inquiries. His shipmates were vague, which made her furious; desertion was bad enough without this male conspiracy of silence. She went to the local police who pointed out that no crime or misdemeanor had been committed as far as they knew, and that it took longer than a missed trip home to prove desertion. Then having grown strong and tall with righteous indignation she went to see the pastor. She suspected him of knowing where her husband was, which in fact he had heard, and she intended to invoke his approval and assistance in her righteous cause. The pastor knew Clara and Harry and Marjorie the daughter. He also knew something about the home situation. He listened while Clara blazed at him in that buzz-saw voice and spat out her wrongs. Finally it was his turn and he asked what she wanted him to do. The answer was prompt: "I want you to find out where he is and make him come home." Was it money, the pastor wanted to know, that worried her? No, she admitted reluctantly that Harry had sent her some money by one of the other fishermen. What, then? She said flatly, "I want him to suffer the way he has made me suffer!"

It interests me how easy it is for all of us to be Christians for an hour or so on Sunday. We change our clothes and our demeanor, and enter a sort of parenthesis which may have little to do with our other life. It can so easily be a world of General Principles accompanied by music, to which we give general assent as any decent person would, but with no sense of personal involvement. There is nothing we have to do about it, really, except to agree that these things are doubtless true and that people ought to be better than they are. I doubt that this woman, threatened and embarrassed by her husband's decision to leave her, thought about her religion at that moment one way or another. She felt Right because her husband had to be wrong and here in this minister was a representative of righteousness who would rally to her cause. I am glad to say that this one did not. Instead he invited her in and sat her down and asked her about things in general. They had not had a good talk in some time which he admitted was his fault in not getting around oftener. How was Marjorie? And had she come to know the new family who had moved in across the street. From Portsmouth, was it?

Gradually they began to talk of other things and some of the hardness went out of her face. There was an interesting and gentle person buried in this woman, he reflected. He wondered what had hurt her so much that she had become bitter and had made enemies of her husband and her child, in order to have opponents she could meet, instead of formless ones inside herself. At the end of the conversation the pastor came back to the subject they had begun with. Harry had not written to say that he was not coming back; he had sent some money and had said nothing at all. There was enough money for present needs. How would it be if Clara and Marjorie were to come to supper that night? Nothing special but enough to feed two more. All right? About six? Good.

And so the miracle slowly began. Gradually Clara began to thaw, found a new interest or two, was in church oftener because she wanted to be. Marjorie looked better, less hidden. It got so that Harry could be mentioned without the name sounding like a swear word. Two or three months had gone by and the money had come in regularly. Then the pastor took the next step. He wrote Harry at the navy yard, told him things were better at home, that Clara had admitted one day with a half-smile that she wondered why Harry had not left home sooner! The reply was immediate. Harry said frankly that he only half believed the reports of the change in Clara, that he did miss Marjorie and his friends, and that he felt guilty about deserting even though he had sent the money. More letters were exchanged until Harry was willing on the assurances of the pastor to take the chance. He and Clara met Harry's train. Marjorie was in school and had been left there purposely. When the train drew in, Harry was one of the first persons to alight. He stood for a moment at the top of the steps searching the people on the platform till his eyes met Clara's. His face relaxed, then he smiled. It seemed years since he had seen her look like that. He guessed it was going to be all right and he was glad that he had come home.

The three of them went to the church, found some coffee and a place to talk. It was slow and shy at first but the pastor helped by telling Harry frankly just what had happened.

After some further three-way talk he left them alone for a while. When he came back he, too, guessed that it was going to be all right. At his suggestion they knelt down and said some prayers, admitting the wrong on both sides and being thankful to God for a new start after all this time. And so the two went home to wait for Marjorie.

Four Elements in Reconciliation

Now it does not always happen like this. Many times the bitterness is drunk like wine, and the enemy stays an enemy forever. But this is the only chance there is. It seems to me that in any case of reconciliation there are four elements. They will have to be stated one after another in writing, but there is no particular order about them. Situations differ, and in a way they all happen at once. But they are all essential. One of them is a willingness to discuss the problem. This is the one we put off as long as we can. Another is a willingness to trust a third party. In the case of Harry and Clara it was the local pastor, but it might be someone else. The advantages are that people often can speak freely to a third person when they cannot at the moment speak to each other. Also, the third person acts as a sort of sounding board —sometimes a referee, sometimes an interpreter, sometimes just as the only possible means of the husband and wife meeting at all. It may be that the threesome will precede the free discussion between husband and wife or it may follow it, the third person being appealed to or agreed upon by both contestants.

Thirdly, for Christians there is the central resource of the Christian faith, the root fact that forgiveness is possible and available. I mean, of course, that each of us can be forgiven, restored into fellowship with God in Christ. This restoration is at the heart of all Christian services of worship, confession, and thanksgiving, and is expressed in the attitude of Christians toward one another. It is the acceptance of his forgiveness in Christ which makes a person a Christian; he practices his Christianity by offering the same gift to others. Everything else in the Christian religion is secondary to this good news, the principle of the Lord's Prayer, that we can be forgiving because we are forgiven. It is amazing how many Christians in marriage difficulties do not realize that the strongest power in the world is theirs to use: the power of forgiveness which is stronger than hate, stronger than fear. This is true partly because we confuse the Christian faith with good works and committees, with moralism and sentimentalism. A Christian is a person who can be forgiven and forgiving, and what better place to start than in "the church which is in thy house." Forgiveness is the highest and holiest gift of God and at the same time the most practical. It is that gift of God which we need most and most often. It is the fabric of our life together as people, it is the daily bread of married life. It does not mean that what you have said or done does not matter; it matters very much and cannot be unsaid or undone. It does mean that what you have said or done can be soaked up by the compassion of the Lord, that you yourself will continue to be held and sustained and loved. And the same priceless gift is offered by husbands and wives to one another and to their children. Forgiveness precedes repentance, makes it possible, breaks down the walls of partition between person and person that they may indeed be one.

The fourth element in reconciliation, and one of the steady considerations of this whole book, derives from the possibility of forgiveness, that is that one can *afford* to be wrong. Not only not right but wrong, and say so. The person who needs always to be right is the person who cannot love because he is pretending, and love never pretends. And he is very difficult to love because he has made a wall of rightness around him. He is desperately protecting his quaking insides by this pretense because he cannot accept love which is a humbling gift. The fact that any one of us is wrong and destructive and unloving a good share of the time is a plain fact. But without love we cannot afford to admit it, to accept it, and to know quite simply that it will happen again. When a person admits to another that he has been wrong, he is taking a chance that the other will agree that such is the case and that is that. But again, it is the only chance there is, the way in which admitted failure can make possible a reciprocal admission of failure and a real meeting occur. People snap at each other and fight each other out of insecurity—fumbling, trying, hurting, loving, hating, reaching out—sometimes finding each other deeply and truly after years of living together because they dropped their defenses and took a chance on the truth. Everybody is insecure and hopes that others will not notice it. After years of fooling a lot of people, a man can sometimes admit to his wife in the middle of the night that he is scared stiff, not scared of meeting a payment on a note but scared of meeting himself. He may make the wonderful discovery that his wife is the one person in the world before whom he does not have to pretend. If so he is a wealthy man. Shared darkness sometimes brings with it the possibility of light or at least of companionship in the dark.

The Old Word for It Is Charity

There is evidence to show that most divorces are entered into reluctantly. Many begin when one party uses it as a threat or a weapon, then finds that something has been set in motion which cannot be stopped. Stubbornness and pride often see it through, even though neither party really wants it. And, to be utterly practical, most couples can't afford it. A marriage, even if not the dream one had, is worth a lot of reaching for, a lot of willingness to be wrong.

Let me offer another illustration which may help. Except for its ending, it might be the substance of a hundred movies or lending library novels. The characters in order of appearance are John, Pat his wife, and his secretary Mary. So far nothing could be more like a stock plot (they are the ones that happen of course; that's why they are "stock"), but the relationships are interesting and may set out in a familiar medium a number of our thoughts so far. All three of these people are good friends, all are college graduates, normal, average Americans. All are active members of the local church. John is thirty years old, tall and lean, pleasant in appearance and manner. He works hard at his job and is doing well at it. He is known and respected in the small city where he has lived now for six years. He plays a good game of tennis or golf, enjoys a hand at bridge. He is friendly and dependable, has a number of friends. John met his wife during his last year in college, married her when she graduated after he had been a year in his present job. Pat, too, is tall and dark, looks well in tailored suits, plays a hard game of tennis, is cool, intelligent, efficient—the sort of person one would want in a difficult situation. She always knows what to do. They have been married for five years and it has been a good marriage. So far they have no children. She is twenty-eight. Mary has been John's secretary for three years and knows her job. She answered an ad in the paper and has become a working member of the office family. She is twenty-four and would like to be married. She is Pat's temperamental opposite. Always neat, she tends to dress informally, lives by herself in a small apartment, collects stray dogs and cats, likes to cook, read, and listen to music. She and Pat frequently have lunch together and there is a standing joke about John and Pat finding an eligible bachelor for her and John's having to find himself a new secretary.

So it is at the beginning of summer when Pat is called home several hundred miles away because her father is seriously sick. There is no question about her going; of course she must go and she will surely be back long before their scheduled vacation time. But her father's sickness drags along for a month. She flies back once, writes frequently, and telephones occasionally. Finally her father dies and Pat, the capable one, is persuaded to stay on for the settling of the estate. Reluctantly, though she enjoys being competent, she does so, and July is almost over before the rather complicated business is completed and she is free to leave.

Meanwhile John, left alone for the longest time since the marriage began, is restless. He has come to depend on Pat's competent way of running the house with no apparent effort and his bachelor housekeeping suffers in comparison. Besides it is June, the trees heavy with leaf, the nights warm and pleasant, and he is lonesome. It is difficult for him to remember when he was not married to Pat, but now she seems very far away. He resents a little the family demands that keep her away so long. He loses buttons, struggles with the laundromat on Saturdays, makes a half-hearted attempt to keep the house clean and orderly. On one of the occasions when he is making a pass at house-cleaning Mary stops by in her little car to bring some papers which need his signature. She takes in the situation at a glance and, over John's feeble protests, rolls up her sleeves and goes to work.

It is pleasant to have a woman in the house again. She makes a merry and purposeful busyness as things begin to take shape. She deals with the buttonless jacket, dumps out the accumulated rubbish, cleans the sink properly, picks some flowers, and makes the record player seem worthwhile again. The place begins to look and feel like home and he is grateful. Mary suggests that with what he has in the refrigerator and what she has at home they could make one decent meal and while John showers she goes home to get it. By the time she comes back bathed and changed, her arms full of things, John has prepared some refreshments and is feeling better than he has felt in a long time. Supper over, they listened to music and talked, finding each other interesting in a new setting. When the records were over they switched to the radio and danced.

Does anyone know to what degree affairs of this kind are consciously planned and what degree is accidental, perhaps prompted by the unconscious? Various persons will give various answers for various reasons. At any rate it did happen and things were different. Life was more interesting for John, at least for the time being, and Mary was radiant. Their conversation at the office took on a different tone, days and nights blending together in memory and prospect. In the old days they used to have lunch together occasionally. Now they did so almost every day and planned the evening together. They had lived on their island in the sea of time for about a month when Pat called one Sunday to say she would be coming in that evening in time for supper, out somewhere she hoped. John put the phone back. "That was Pat," he said unnecessarily. "Yes. Tonight." After a bit of not too comfortable silence they began to talk about what they had to talk about. What to do? Each of them had given the question considerable thought when alone, but had avoided coming to any conclusion. Now it seemed they would have to. As they got down to it there appeared to be three possibilities: they could go on and say nothing; they could stop and say nothing; they could stop and tell Pat. Neither of them even named the possibility of divorce, with or without remarriage. They parted uneasily without having concluded anything.

It was a sleepless night for Mary. She was at the office next morning when John arrived, neither of them looking their best. She came to John's desk and asked softly, "Did you tell her?" "Yes," said John, "I had to." Mary's mouth opened soundlessly, her hand at her throat. Finally she managed, "What did she say?" "She didn't say much of anything," John replied miserably. The telephone rang. John picked it up nervously, then with relief found he was talking to a business associate. It was a difficult morning and at lunch time John and Mary, by tacit agreement, ate separately.

Pat was shattered. She *had* been gone a long time, too long she now realized with a pang, but she wouldn't have believed that John . . . and Mary. Why, Mary had written her several times. What a ghastly homecoming. She had known that something was wrong as soon as she looked at John. He was all tight around the mouth and his voice wasn't right. Halfway through supper she had asked him what was the matter and he had told her. They had gone home in silence. The house seemed strange. There were some records on the hi-fi that were not theirs. Mary's she supposed. It was a bad night. Each of them was up once or twice, but the conversation was not resumed. John went out quietly without breakfast. Pat came down to the kitchen and made some coffee. It tasted awful. After thinking in circles for what seemed a long time she called the rector of the parish, the person who had married them five years ago, a good friend who had often been in their home. He was glad to hear that she was back, told her of course he would see her. She walked to the church; it wasn't far and she felt the need of some exercise. The rector welcomed her warmly, saw that something was wrong and heard her out. At the end of the brief recital Pat made no attempt to hold back the tears, said, "Well, I guess this is the end for John and me. Thanks for listening." He persuaded her to stay a while and they talked of other things but without much heart.

After lunch John called the same person from a pay phone, said he had to see him as soon as possible. The rector told him to come at once, added that Pat had already been there. "Then you know?" "Yes, I know, so come along." John told his story, sparing himself nothing; finally said, "What a fool I have been to ruin the best thing I have ever known." The clergyman suggested that John come back that evening and bring Pat. "Come for supper," he added, thinking of avoiding another silent meal for them. "Maybe she won't come," said John. "Maybe not. I'll ask her." They did come. There were six of them including two teen-age children who were glad to see Pat. The conversation was not brilliant but at least it was conversation and it was real. After supper John and Pat followed the rector into the study and found chairs. He said a few words about them and their marriage and their home, a little about Mary and the long separation, then waited for them to speak.

It was not an easy conversation. John plunged in, said what he had said before to the rector, added that when Pat had called he could not decide whether to tell her or not; but as soon as he had seen her he knew he had to because he loved her. Pat admitted her deep hurt, said she did not hate Mary, at least not much, regretted the long absence. And so it went. After a while they were talking to each other as if they were alone in the room and as they had not since Pat had come home. Finally Pat walked over and sat on the arm of her husband's chair. She found his hand, looked at him steadily, said, "John, I can be hurt and you can be hurt but *we* can't be hurt." John took her in his arms and burst into tears. And the miracle of forgiveness and restoration took place. The worst part was still to come, the days and nights of living it out, the chance that it might flare up again. But the first big barrier had been crossed. They said some prayers of confession and thanksgiving and went home together. The rector did some praying after they had gone.

There was still the question of Mary to be dealt with. She was the expendable woman, the woman without status. The pastor went to see her, told her gently what had happened and heard her out. The next day he suggested a bold course to Pat who after some consideration accepted it. She invited Mary to Sunday night supper—there had been many such times together in the last three years—and impressed her that she really wanted her to come. John and the rector also urged her to accept. Things had not been easy at the office. Mary did accept. She came in tentatively, almost shyly. Pat had made up her mind what she was going to do, and in her characteristically forthright style she got it over with. She said that she had been badly hurt and that it would take her a long time to get over it, but that she and John had met again and a part of the fault for the whole thing had been hers for staying away so long. She would not pretend that she had liked what had happened, but she did at least partly understand it and she wanted Mary to understand that she did not hate her. She got no farther because it was Mary's turn to burst into tears and it was Pat's arms that were around her. Not long after, Mary found another job and moved to another city. John and Pat saw her off together.

Once again, it does not always happen this way, perhaps not often. But it does happen, and when it does the elements of reconciliation we have noted will be there. In the case of John and Pat we have two Christians with some maturity and some knowledge of the resources open to them, including a usable third party. But the foundation of their reconciliation is the knowledge of the power of forgiveness, and their use of it in smaller ways during their married life together. Most major decisions in life have case histories; they do not happen simply as splendid or terrible isolated events. Divorce is the legal recognition that a marriage has failed, but the disintegration of the marriage began a year or two before this conclusion. Similarly, a great act of forgiveness is unlikely unless preceded by a history of smaller forgivings, the daily give and take of two loving, fumbling human beings.

Love is a mode of knowledge. We know by loving and we may love by knowing. Self-love is idolatry. The deep ample generous love of another person—the old word for it is charity—partakes of the love of God for all of us. It is a great blessing that such love is open to us on pilgrimage. It is our joy in time of harmony, our help in time of trouble. "Love's not time's fool"; it is tough enough to bear a lot of pain, and it goes always on light feet. One of the achievements of a real marriage is, in Chesterton's felicitous phrase, "to enter the heart without knocking."

Prayers

Prayers

For an Engaged Couple

O Holy Jesus, who blessed with thy presence the wedding feast at Cana; Bless us who are preparing to be joined in the bond of marriage. Give us serenity in our hearts, honesty with each other, and devotion to thee, that we may find strength in time of trouble, patience in time of trial, and joy in companionship all our days.

At a Wedding Rehearsal

Behold and bless us, O God, gathered here in thy Name and presence: this bride and this groom, those who attend them, their families and friends. Help us to understand the blessings of thy love, and give us reverent hearts and minds as we prepare for the sacrament of Christian marriage.

For a Married Couple

O God of love and tenderness and strength, who hast joined our purposes and made us one flesh; go with us in all our ways; Bless our home and our love, our comings and our goings; make us worthy of each other's best; comfort us in trouble, sustain us in the hour of self-distrust, and knit our lives together in the good companionship of thy Son, Jesus Christ our Lord.

Blessing of a Home

Our heavenly Father, fill this home with the gladness of thy presence. Bless all who live here with thy gift of love, and help us to show it forth, to each other and to all men. Keep us safe from all evil and bring us to thy heavenly kingdom; through Jesus Christ our Lord.

For One Who Is Pregnant

O God, who art the well-spring of life, I bless thee for the mystery of creation hidden in my body; give me patience and cheerfulness while my baby grows, and a quiet mind in which to give thee thanks.

Birth of a Child

Unto thee, O God, we offer our thanksgivings for the miracle of birth and for the joy of bringing a new life into thy world. Bless us, we beseech thee, with wisdom and patience in the nurture of our child whom we welcome in thy Name; through Jesus Christ our Lord.

For One Who Has Lost a Child at Birth

I give thanks unto thee, O Lord God, heavenly Father, through Jesus Christ, thy dear Son, that thou hast been so graciously present with me in all my needs; and even though the heavy burden of sorrow has come so soon upon me, still thou dost grant me the comforting assurance that all things work together for good to them that love thee. O most merciful Father, I humbly offer thee my love and trust and tenderly commit the soul of my little one into thy keeping against the day when we shall be united in thy presence. And I beseech thee, take not the comfort of thy Spirit from me, but grant me grace ever to learn and to do thy will; through Jesus Christ, thy Son, our Lord.

A Child at Baptism

O God our Father, we thank thee for our child, (N); and as we take *him* to *his* baptism in thy holy Church we pray thee to receive *him* into the arms of thy love and to keep *him* ever in thy watchful care. Give us grace to help *him* grow in grace, both by our own good example and by instruction in the teachings of the Church, and may *he* remain a faithful soldier and servant of our Lord Jesus Christ to *his* life's end.

On the Adoption of a Child

Our Father, who hast bestowed upon us this great privilege of taking to ourselves as one of our own one of thy little ones, to love and care for, and to bring up in thy faith and fear; Grant us, we pray thee, the grace to give to *him* the full measure of our devotion, and to set before *him* always a good example of Christian life. Bless us in our growth together, and may our home be enriched in the simple joys that come of loving and serving one another; through Jesus Christ our Lord.

For Our Child's Birthday

O God, our Father, bless our child and keep *him* safe all the days of *his* life; grant *him* good friends, happy memories, and a thankful heart to praise thy Name; through Jesus Christ our Lord.

A Sick Child

O God, who knowest the needs of all thy children, help and bless our sick child, we beseech thee; give *him* courage and patience, bless the doctors and all who minister to *him* of thy healing gifts, and restore *him* to health and strength; through Jesus Christ our Lord.

For the Parents of a Retarded Child

O God of mercy and compassion, behold and bless us in our need; fold our child in the arms of thy love; take away all bitterness from our hearts and give us patience, kindness, and wisdom to choose wisely for our child who is a whole person in thy sight; in the name of Jesus Christ our Saviour.

Death of a Child

O God, whose most dear Son did take little children into his arms and bless them; Give us grace, we beseech thee, to entrust the soul of this child to thy never-failing care and love, and bring us all to thy heavenly kingdom, through the same Jesus Christ our Lord.

For a Child Who Seems to Be Making a Wrong Choice

O God, our only source of wisdom and strength, who hast given us the joy and responsibility of the nurture of children; Watch with our child, we beseech thee, who seems to be making a wrong choice. Grant that whatever of the truth we have taught *him* may stay with *him* to guide *him;* help us to do neither too much nor too little, and keep *him* in thy holy keeping; through Jesus Christ our Lord.

On a Wedding Anniversary

Heavenly Father, we give thee hearty thanks for the day when we were made one in holy matrimony, for thy blessing upon us then and for thy continual mercies until now. We thank thee that our love has deepened with the passing days and for all the joys of our home and family life. Renew thy blessing upon us now, we beseech thee, as we renew our vows of love and loyalty; and may thy Holy Spirit strengthen us that we may ever remain steadfast in our faith and in thy service; through Jesus Christ our Lord.

In Time of Monotony

O God, our Father, who knowest that we cannot always be merry, sustain us, we beseech thee, when life seems dull and drab and without color; help us to remember better times and to look forward confidently to a renewal of spirit; through the serenity of thy Son, Jesus Christ our Lord.

A Happy Home

O God, our Father, we thank thee for our home and family; for love and forbearance, for friends and foes, for laughter enjoyed and sorrow shared, for the daily bread of thy bounty in good times and bad. Help us to be mindful of thy gifts and glad to show forth thy praise; through Jesus Christ our Lord.

In Time of Tension

O God, our Father, who knowest all thy children, help us with thy wisdom to understand ourselves and each other; melt our pride with the warmth of thy redeeming charity and take us back to the days of our loving trust, that we may build again in the good companionship of Jesus Christ our Lord.

A Death in the Family

Grant, O Lord, to all who are bereaved the spirit of faith and courage, that they may have strength to meet the days to come with steadfastness and patience; not sorrowing as those without hope, but in thankful remembrance of thy great goodness through the years, and in sure expectation of a joyful reunion with those they love; and this we ask in the Name of Jesus Christ our Lord.

On One Leaving Home

O God, who art in every place beholding the evil and the good; Take into thine own keeping our dear one now going into the world of strangers. Give *him* courage, prudence, self-control. Grant *him* a right judgment in all things. Raise up for *him* friends, if it be thy will, and deliver *him* from the snares and sorrows of loneliness by the power and joy of thy presence. Grant that in every place *he* may find the House of God and the gate of heaven. Safeguard *him* with the ministry of thy never-failing providence, now and always; for the sake of Jesus Christ our Lord.

For Those We Love

O God, whose fatherly care reachest to the uttermost parts of the earth; We humbly beseech thee to behold and bless those whom we love, now absent from us. Defend them from all dangers of soul and body; and grant that both they and we, drawing nearer to thee, may be bound together in the communion of thy Holy Spirit, and in the fellowship of thy saints; through Jesus Christ our Lord.

For Our Needs

Almighty God, the fountain of all wisdom, who knowest our necessities before we ask, and our ignorance in asking; We beseech thee to have compassion upon our infirmities; and those things which for our unworthiness we dare not, and for our blindness we cannot ask, vouchsafe to give us, for the worthiness of thy Son Jesus Christ our Lord.

Serenity

God grant me
The serenity to accept the things I cannot change,
The courage to change the things I can,
And the wisdom to distinguish the one from the other.